UNIX
Communications
and Networking

UNIX
Communications
and Networking

■ ■ ■

By Kevin Reichard
and David Burnette

MIS:PRESS

A Subsidiary of
Henry Holt and Co., Inc.

First Edition—1994

Printed in the United States of America.

Library of Congress CIP Data

Reichard, Kevin.
    UNIX Communications and Networking/By Kevin Reichard and David
    Burnette
       p.   cm.
    ISBN 1-55828-388-9 : $19.95
    Includes index.
    1. UNIX (Computer file) 2. Computer networks. 3. Operating systems
(Computers)   I. Burnette, David. II. Title.
QA76.76.063R4437   1994   94-32471
004.6—dc20   CIP

10 9 8 7 6 5 4 3 2 1

MIS:Press books are available at special discounts for bulk purchases for sales promotions, premiums, fund-raising, or educational use. Special editions or book excerpts can also be created to specification.

For details contact: Special Sales Director
                       MIS:Press
                       a subsidiary of Henry Holt and Company, Inc.
                       115 West 18th Street
                       New York, New York 10011

Managing Editor: Cary Sullivan   Assoc. Production Editor: Erika Putre
Development Editor: Laura Lewin   Technical Editor: Eric Johnson
Production Editor: Anne Alessi   Copy Editor: Suzanne Ingrao

▪ TABLE OF CONTENTS ▪

▼

▼

▪ INTRODUCTION ▪

Welcome to *UNIX Communications and Networking!* This book covers one of the hottest topics in the UNIX world—as well as popular culture as a whole: having your computer call my computer.

Much of this interest in communications lies in the incredible rise of the Internet as a cultural agent. And while the jury is still out regarding the ultimate future of the Internet—will cable television render it unnecessary someday? Will it collapse under the weight of a huge user base who cringe at paying their freight?—it's clear that the Internet has touched a larger nerve in our society: The need to connect to others all around the world and have information within easy reach.

But there's more to UNIX communications than the Internet, which is why only one chapter of nine in this book actually covers the Internet. UNIX was built from the ground up to facilitate networking and communications; commands that let you communicate with other users on your own system and beyond are built directly into the UNIX operating system. Hence, this book.

▼

Who Should Read This Book?

This book is meant for the pure UNIX beginner: Someone who was thrown in front of a UNIX terminal for various reasons (job changes, upgrades in the computer system) and were told, by hook or by crook, that they would master the UNIX operating system in general, and communications specifically. That includes:

- ▲ Beginning UNIX users who found that communicating with the home office in Sioux City, Iowa, via electronic mail was a prime component of the job.

- ▲ Experienced UNIX users who were told that their job security rested on how well they mastered the Internet.

- ▲ Computer users who are looking for a painless way to connect with the Internet and are using UNIX for this purpose.

- ▲ System administrators who were told by their bosses to get the company on the Internet by next week.

In short, it's anyone who uses UNIX, networking, and communications.

With this kind of audience in mind, this book was written taking nothing for granted in terms of experience and expertise. Beginning UNIX concepts—even those with direct counterparts in the DOS world—are explained on a very basic level. Elemental networking concepts, such as the basic act of finding out who's on the corporate network, are explained fully. In addition, you're not only told how things work—you're told why things work the way they do, so that you can take this information to your specific job situation and apply it to your circumstances.

Command Comparisons

When a new UNIX command is introduced, you'll also find a Command Reference within the same section. These references exist for two reasons:

They summarize the main points from the text, and they also are designed to stand out when you inevitably return to the text to review information about a command or procedure. The Command Reference will use the same layout throughout the book:

▲ **Command syntax** This details exactly how you use the command.

▲ **Purpose** One or two sentences summarize what the command does.

▲ **Options** Virtually every command features options, which change the way the command works.

Since some of the UNIX commands have rather lengthy lists of options—including many options that are rarely used—some discretion was used when compiling lists of commands and options. You shouldn't assume that the listings of options cover every possible option; otherwise, this book would have been even bigger than it is now. If you're interested in complete command references, check Appendix A for a listing of UNIX reference works.

Examples in This Book

There are many examples used within this book to illuminate concepts and practices. With every UNIX system being different, there's the real danger that the examples cannot be used by every UNIX end user. However, always remember that even if the specific example isn't applicable to your specific situation, the general concepts behind the example are applicable to the vast majority of UNIX systems. For instance, something as mundane as logging in a UNIX system varies from system to system. However, virtually every UNIX system requires some form of a login procedure. In this instance, what's important is not the actual set of keystrokes that logs you in a system, but the procedure of logging in a system and the concepts behind the need for logins.

Icons

Important UNIX concepts and commands are highlighted with icons from the artist John Bush (who is also responsible for the illustrations at the beginning of each chapter). There are several different icons used:

This icon points out where a UNIX command is introduced and explained.

This icon highlights an important fact or concept.

This icon tells you not to worry about why things work—just that they should work.

This icon explains a more technical issue.

▼

Conventions Used in This Book

Many of the things discussed in this book will be confusing to you, and sometimes the way books are laid out adds to the confusion. We've attempted to create a very user-friendly book to help you wade through the very confusing world of UNIX computing. Some of the things we've done include:

▲ Commands that are to be typed directly into the UNIX system are indicated by the `monospaced` font.

▲ Keystrokes—that is, keys you press as part of your UNIX system usage, such as the **Enter** key—are indicated by the **bold** type.

▲ Filenames and directories are also in **bold** type.

▲ Machine names and electronic-mail addresses are marked by the *italic* type.

▲ New concepts are introduced and highlighted in **bold** type.

UNIX Fundamentals

This book is one in a series of books from MIS:Press, UNIX Fundamentals, dedicated toward UNIX end users. This series is an ambitious attempt to explain the UNIX operating system in terms the average end user can handle. This is more of a project than you might think—the vast majority of offerings in the UNIX-book world center around advanced technical information for system administrators and UNIX gurus.

If you find yourself curious about UNIX after reading this book, you should check out some of the other titles in the series. The first title, *UNIX Basics*, covers the UNIX operating system from the ground up. Other titles in the series focus on UNIX concepts for DOS/*Windows* users and UNIX freeware/shareware.

▼

Acknowledgments

Many people were central in bringing this book to your hands:

- ▲ Laura Lewin, a very patient editor who is responsible for the look and feel of the entire series; she deserves far more credit than she'll ever receive for bringing this book (and, indeed, the UNIX Fundamentals series) to a successful publication
- ▲ Nelson King, MIS:Press author and a frequent coffee companion whose sagacious advice helped shape this work
- ▲ The members of the CompuServe UNIX Forum (particularly George L. Smythe and Caroll Ford), who provide a very useful window in the world of UNIX users

Feedback

We would love to hear your comments about this book—good, bad, or ugly. You can send us mail via the Internet at *reichard@mrnet.net*. If you have a CompuServe account, you can drop us a note there (the account number is 73670,3422). Or, if your UNIX system is not connected to the Internet, you can drop us a line in care of MIS:Press, 115 W. 18th St., New York City, NY 10011.

▪ CHAPTER ONE ▪

Introducing E-Mail and Networking

Electronic communication is over a century old, beginning with the telegraph, and perhaps older still if you consider the French and Swedish optical telegraphs in the late 1700s and 1800s. Thankfully, modern electronic communication is much speedier, reliable, and easier to use than past incarnations. Topics in this chapter include:

- ▲ A description of what e-mail is.
- ▲ The advantages of e-mail.
- ▲ What a network is.
- ▲ An overview of the pending information superhighway.
- ▲ Why UNIX is important to e-mail and networking.
- ▲ A brief description of the UNIX operating system.
- ▲ A definition of electronic mail.
- ▲ Electronic mail and networks.
- ▲ How to contact the authors.

▼

Welcome to the Void

Whether you've realized it or not, you've probably already encountered some form of electronic mail or networking. Take the automated teller machines dotting our urban landscape, for example. Every time you use your ATM card, you're plugging into a network of banks, computers, and databases. Granted, this network is limited in what it can do, but it performs a handful of very specific (and very helpful) functions very well. In offices (and the homes of some computer enthusiasts), networks perform much more varied tasks but essentially serve the same purpose: connecting computers together so that they can share data.

E-mail, short for electronic mail, has been around for many years but recently has experienced a phenomenal growth in popularity. Its earliest incarnation was perhaps the telegraph. Though not nearly as fast or easy to use as today's e-mail systems, the telegraph and their operators transmitted messages between distant locations electronically. Today, telephone lines, microwave relay stations, and satellites have replaced telegraph poles and wires. Instead of specially trained operators, you and your computer send messages on their way.

The so-called information superhighway is not yet real nor will it be for some time. Like the American freeway system, the information superhighway will take many years to build, cost a lot of money, and fundamentally alter the environment, though in this case the environment isn't so much physical as it is electronic. Until that glorious day when the Infobahn connects everyone in the global village, we have the Internet, with which you are probably familiar.

The Internet is not some mystical land entered only with the permission of arcane priests and the correct incantations (though it once may have been). In reality, the Internet is a collection of many thousands of computers, most of them running some form of UNIX, that had its humble origins in a network connecting universities and government research centers.

Now, anyone with a computer and a modem can wade into the information sea that is the 'Net. It would be pointless to quote current statistics on the size of the Internet or the projections on how large it will be in a year. Suffice it to say that the limits to the extraordinary growth of this communications medium have not yet been realized.

UNIX is a Many-Splendored Thing

Networking is as much a part of UNIX as the C programming language, lowercase letters, or Birkenstocks. Soon after Sun Microsystems released its first computer, it decided to provide built-in networking as a standard feature in all its machines. Sun's slogan was prophetic—"The network is the computer"—something Sun has proven during the 12 years since its founding.

The Internet is at the large-scale end of UNIX communications. Toward the smaller end is the local area network, or LAN. PCs, Macintoshes, and UNIX machines can all be networked together. Unlike the Internet, LANs aren't closely tied to UNIX. Though non-UNIX machines can access the Internet, to do so typically requires connecting to a UNIX machine first and then launching out into the electronic Void.

UNIX is as varied as it is powerful. It is the only operating system running on a range of hardware, from PCs to Cray supercomputers. Long a bastion of the technical computing arena—the folks who design integrated circuits or develop software—many UNIX vendors are hoping to infiltrate the commercial sector next. They hope to replace the IBM mainframes and minicomputers, claimed to be in the descendant by pundits and analysts of the media, with tidy UNIX boxes networked together in happy communion.

Several years ago, there were rumored to be over 200 different versions of UNIX. Thankfully, UNIX has converged over the years to a few major versions, with the faint possibility that even these could one day evolve into one. Despite the different flavors of UNIX, there is a core set of communications utilities and functionality that most possess, and it is these that will be the focus of this book.

No matter how you might encounter UNIX, one of the tasks you will likely find yourself performing is communicating with someone else, either locally, at a distance, or maybe even at an unknown location. If CompuServe is the extent of your computer communications experience, hang on—you're in for a wild, chaotic journey of data streams and internetwork packets.

When everything works well, e-mail is a wonderful thing, far faster than normal postal mail or even Federal Express. A letter traveling from Los Angeles to New York via e-mail can arrive in about a minute. At best, the U.S. Postal Service can deliver this letter in two days. Private carriers such as Federal Express can cut this in half. Facsimile transmission can shave this still further to a minute or so, but faxes convert textual and graphical information into a form that is not easily interpreted by a computer.

A fax arrives either as a printed page or, if fax software is used to receive the transmission, a data file that is difficult to convert back into a form similar to that which is sent. Optical character recognition is getting better, but it will always be less than perfect. To ensure complete accuracy of transmission, speed, and reliability, nothing beats e-mail.

Cost is another matter. The initial set-up costs for an e-mail connection can run into several hundred dollars, if you count the modems, phone lines, communication software, and service providers that connect you to the Net. Typically, this is an up-front cost, however, and monthly maintenance fees can be as low as $10 or even drop to the cost of a long-distance phone call if a direct computer-to-computer connection is used.

Some Terms

Don't be afraid. As with many new fields, the biggest hurdle is understanding the vocabulary. Fortunately, the vocabulary for e-mail and networking is fairly simple and straightforward, and it is probably something to which you've already been exposed. LAN, Internet, and e-mail were all words that didn't exist 10 years ago. Now they are becoming commonplace in nightly news broadcasts and police reports. The age of electronic textual communication is here, and if you work in any sort of modern office, you're probably already a part of it.

First things first: **e-mail** is a document transmitted electronically from one computer to another is e-mail, whether it be a simple text file, an image stored in one of the many computer formats available, a spreadsheet file, or anything else that a computer can send and receive. For example, this manuscript was communicated from author to editor via e-mail. It did not exist in printed form until it was ready to be copy-edited by patient professionals in New York.

A **LAN**, or local area network, is a collection of two or more computers connected together electronically, usually by wire. Over this wire, the machines can exchange data, share resources such as printers and modems, or even share the resources of each other. One of corporate marketing's buzzwords is **client/server**, which is the process by which an application, such as a spreadsheet, is split between the computer that displays the matrix of cells and the computer that performs the calculations and manages the spreadsheet's data. More elaborate divisions of labor are possible with client/server applications, but the most important aspect is that however they are split, the parts typically communicate over a LAN.

Ethernet is the most common communication medium. Just as radio signals must be sent in a special format for receivers to be able to recreate the original audio information that was transmitted, ethernet is the means by which most data is sent by one UNIX computer and correctly received by another. It is a way that data signals are encoded for transmission between computer systems. The cable connecting computers together in a LAN can be viewed as the ether through which data is transmitted, hence the name ethernet.

On the Edge

Children born in the Nineties will ask their parents, "What was it like before the Internet?" just as quizzically as thirtysomethings asked their parents, "What was it like before television?"

Several large magazine publishing firms are already exploring ways to effectively deliver their once-printed material by means of e-mail. Not only is such a feat an answered prayer of environmentalists but it presents the opportunity to provide up-to-the-second information directly to subscribers without the need for a sluggish intermediary, such as the U.S. Postal Service.

▼

> ## ▲ L E A R N   M O R E   A B O U T ▲
>
> The following chapters will tell you all you need to know to send messages, files, and images to anyone whose e-mail address you happen to know, and even some you don't. Also, you'll find out how to crawl around both your local network and the far-flung expanse of the Internet, sampling what these interconnected systems have to offer.

One final word. Given that this is the e-mail age and that this is a book on e-mail, if, at any time, you have a question or comment, send us a note. We can be reached at *reichard@mr.net*. (You'll find out how to send us a message in the next chapter.)

This Chapter in Review

▲ E-mail isn't as new as you might think. The telegraph is an early example of electronic communications technology.

▲ Neither is networking. It's as old as dirt, in computer terms, originating in the early eighties.

▲ UNIX is what makes the Internet possible. Thousands of UNIX computers comprise the Internet.

▲ UNIX is important to networking, too. Machines running UNIX were among the first to adopt networking technology as an important asset in a distributed world.

▲ Ethernet is the method for much UNIX communications.

▲ E-mail is as much evolved beyond paper mail as humans are beyond the amoebae. Replacing the delivery of paper-based documents is a noble, ultimate goal of e-mail, whether it be books, magazines, or other printer material.

▲ At some point, you'll be comfortable enough in your UNIX communications usage to contact the authors of this book. The electronic-mail address is *reichard@mr.net*.

▼

▪ CHAPTER TWO ▪
E-Mail for the Uninitiated

An e-mail message's address is as important as a postal address. It instructs a computer where and how to deliver your message. The message itself is composed of two parts: the header and the message body. Topics in this chapter include:

- ▲ Origins of UNIX e-mail.
- ▲ Today's UNIX electronic mail.
- ▲ Address formulas.
- ▲ How to convert between Usenet and Internet styles of addressing.
- ▲ The paths to true nirvana via Usenet addressing.
- ▲ The advantages to Internet addressing.
- ▲ Your mailbox.
- ▲ The anatomy of an e-mail message.
- ▲ What a mail reader does.
- ▲ How the system tells you that mail has arrived.
- ▲ An introduction to different mail packages within UNIX.

Instant Messages, Instant Mail

E-mail is to postal mail as a Formula-1 racing car is to a Volkswagen Beetle. There is no comparison other than to say that they're both cars. With e-mail, it's fair to say that both electronic mail and postal mail are forms of communication and share a few parts in common.

As mentioned in Chapter 1, the first form of e-mail was probably the telegraph, but in all honesty that's stretching it a bit. The first instance of what can be considered modern-day UNIX e-mail was created in the early 1970s by Dennis Ritchie and Ken Thompson when they wrote the first version of what would become the UNIX operating system. This piece of software was designed to run on the modern computer of the day: a Digital Equipment Corp. PDP-7. Today's personal computers are more powerful than the PDP-7, but in its day the PDP-7 was a state-of-the-art computer and a perfect receptacle for a state-of-the-art operating system—and e-mail.

The virtues of UNIX e-mail are manifold, but the most prominent are its effortlessness, immediacy, and cost, both in economic and environmental terms. If you can hack out barely coherent sentences in the language of your choice on a computer keyboard, you're capable of sending e-mail. That the greatest physical effort required to send a message is the typing of characters is perhaps e-mail's greatest feature. There is no need to lick and seal an envelope, affix a stamp, or even to scrawl out an address for the hoped-for recipient of your fine prose. With e-mail, all you need to do is finger-peck a paragraph and hit the **Return** key. Chances are the computer systems between you and your addressee will do the rest. You can invoke some bells and whistles, of course, but in its simplest form, that is all there is to UNIX e-mail.

Address Formulas

For your letter to get from you to its intended recipient, you must correctly address it. Most e-mail addresses today are relatively simple, compared to what they once were. Undoubtedly, you've heard of the Internet and all its concomitant benefits. The Internet established a style of e-mail addressing that has become the dominant form for e-mail correspondence.

Before the Internet exploded on the scene, however, a loose assemblage of computers running UNIX formed Usenet. Largely run by universities, which is where many UNIX sites were located, Usenet provided a means for thousands of people to exchange e-mail and netnews, a sort of anarchic bulletin board system that is still popular today. Thousands of systems are connected to the primary university networks via phone lines and modems.

The style of e-mail addresses on the Usenet is quite different from addresses used on the Internet, and it is important to be able distinguish between them and convert from one to the other.

The best way to show you the two styles of addressing is with an example. Take an address: *reichard@mr.net.* This is the Internet form. The Usenet form might look something like *uunet!mr.net!reichard*, which is the full path of the address. We say "might" look something like this because Usenet requires the sender of a message to bear quite a bit of the addressing burden borne by the Internet and its interconnected computers and networks.

The Usenet addresses listed in this chapter are not valid, so don't try and send mail to them.

The Internet form uses an @ character to separate parts of the address, while the Usenet form uses several exclamation marks (!) characters to denote the elements of the address. In both cases, the elements separated by the @ and ! characters are network nodes, whether on the Internet

▼

or Usenet. These nodes are often specific computers but sometimes are groups of computers that share the responsibility of forwarding e-mail traffic directly into recipients or onto other nodes for eventual delivery.

In the above Usenet address, *uunet* and *netcom.com* are nodes, and *uunet* and *mr.net* being names for collections of machines whose sole purpose in life is to route and deliver e-mail. It is possible, however, that another Usenet path exists to the mailbox on *mr.net*. It might be *basis!ucbvax!mr.net!reichard*. In this case, you would need access to the machine called *basis* to send a message.

You can see the downside of Usenet addressing: It requires that you know the precise path your e-mail message will take to get from your computer to the recipient. The good side is that there can be many possible routes to a given destination—you just have to find them.

There are two primary forms of e-mail addresses: the Usenet form and the Internet form. The Internet form is now dominant, but before it appeared on the scene, the Usenet form held sway.

Converting between the Usenet and Internet styles of addresses is simple, as you have only to keep in mind the special characters involved, ! for Usenet and @ for Internet, and the order in which components of an address are parsed for each style. With Usenet, the list of nodes or sites is in the order that the mail message will follow as it wends its way toward its final destination. With Internet, the address is not only much simpler, but works in reverse. The recipient's name is first, followed by the destination site.

For example, take the previously mentioned address: *beast!uunet!mr.net!reichard*. This Usenet form lists the exact path e-mail will travel from the sender on *mr.net* to the recipient. The Internet form of this address is *reichard@mr.net*. Much simpler, right? The ! characters have been replaced by the @ character, and the *mr.net* and *reichard* have been juggled around. The Internet style of addressing is easier and, in a way, more elegant than the old Usenet style.

U*unet* have been dropped entirely when switching from Usenet to Internet address forms, for they are no longer needed. Specifying *mr.net* as the destination node is sufficient for e-mail to reach the mailbox for *reichard*. Achieving this simplicity requires that the various nodes on the Internet have unique names. There is only one *mr.net*, for instance.

These names are called **domain names**, and as you see more and more addresses you'll see them fall into categories. The *.net* designation means that *netcom* is a network provider. Other extensions, or top-level domains as they're called in Internet parlance, are *.edu* for educational institutions, *.gov* for government sites, various (such as *.uk* for the United Kingdom) for countries, *.mil* for military installations, and *.com* for commercial enterprises.

A central agency, the Network Information Center (NIC), is the keeper of all the domain names for the Internet. New domain names must be registered with the NIC before they can be used, which ensures that duplicates don't creep into the system and cause havoc.

Your Mailbox

When e-mail gets delivered to a person, a computer doesn't just pop up and hand the person a letter. Instead, the computer puts the message in a file to which the user has access. This file is the person's **mailbox**. New messages don't overwrite old messages. Instead, the new messages are tacked onto the end of your mailbox, with older messages at the beginning and newer ones toward the end.

Your mailbox usually lives in a directory called **/usr/mail** or **/var/spool/mail** and is named after your account name. For instance, if your username is *celeste*, your mailbox would be **/usr/mail/celeste** or **/var/spool/mail/celeste**, or a file called **celeste** in whatever directory your system keeps its mailboxes.

To read messages in your mailbox, you can use any of several mail-reader programs available today. Don't fret if you haven't bought one of the commercially available mail readers. UNIX comes with a few of its own. These might not be as fancy as the commercially available ones, but they get the job done. The next chapter discusses standard mail readers that ship with different versions of UNIX.

The Anatomy of an E-Mail Message

E-mail messages under UNIX are made up of two components: the **header** and the **body**. The header consumes the first 10 or so lines of the message, and the remainder is the body, or the message text itself. The header provides useful information to the programs that manipulate the message in transit and when it finally gets to your mailbox. It is created by the computers that handle the message enroute, and indicates the path by which the e-mail traveled to your door.

Figure 2.1 contains an e-mail message chronicling the unfortunate accident of a computer columnist.

```
From snert@sunrise.East.Sun.COM Thu Jan 27 20:57:19 1994
  Return-Path: <snert@sunrise.East.Sun.COM>
Received: from Sun.COM by mr.net (4.1/SMI-4.1)
  id AA19299; Thu, 27 Jan 94 20:57:19 PST
Received: from snail.Sun.COM (snail.Corp.Sun.COM) by Sun.COM
  (4.1/SMI-4.1) id AA08126; Thu, 27 Jan 94 20:58:00 PST
Received: from East.Sun.COM by snail.Sun.COM (4.1/SMI-4.1)
  id AA15828; Thu, 27 Jan 94 20:57:57 PST
Received: from sunrise.East.Sun.COM by East.Sun.COM (4.1/SMI-4.1)
  id AA03865; Thu, 27 Jan 94 23:57:54 EST
Received: by sunrise.East.Sun.COM (4.1/SMI-4.1-900117)
  id AA15061; Thu, 27 Jan 94 23:57:46 EST
Date: Thu, 27 Jan 94 23:57:46 EST
From: snert@sunrise.East.Sun.COM (Hal Snert - NE Area Systems Engineer)
Message-Id: <9401280457.AA15061@sunrise.East.Sun.COM>
To: reichard@mr.net
Subject: ice 1, volvo 0

today i proved just how badly our volvo wagon handles in the snow.
driving from my in-laws into work, i hit a patch of ice, lost control
of the rear of the car, skidded into the oncoming traffic lane, back
```

into my lane, turned sideways, and ended up finally getting enough
traction to shoot off the side of the road. the road had a nice
6-foot gully next to it, lined with trees. i went into the gully,
hit a tree with the driver's side headlight, spun the car around
again, hit another tree with the rear taillight/quarter panel, and
came to rest perpendicular to the road. i left lights, trim, grilles,
and my front bumper on the road/ditch/tree bark.

it's been 7 years and 2 days since my last accident.

—hal

FIGURE 2.1 An example of an e-mail message

The header is obvious by its unreadability; the accident text follows. Some elements are visible in the header, such as the *From:* and *To:* lines. As the names suggest, these are the sender and recipient of the e-mail message.

Probably the most useful of the header's lines is the *Subject:* line. Though not required, the sender usually has the option of filling in the subject field of an outgoing e-mail message.

Like the subject line of an office memo, you can use an e-mail's *Subject:* line to indicate the topic of the message that follows. The task of wading through hundreds of e-mail messages at a time is made much easier by performing some sort of triage based upon what each purports to contain. Mail form your dentist can be blissfully skipped, while an urgent note from your manager summoning you to her office might best be read first.

The *Received:* lines are added by each computer as it receives the message along its journey. You can see machine names and dates of receipt amid the computerese that composes much of the header. The *Return-Path:* is exactly that—the return address for the message. Figure 2.1 contains a message transmitted over the Internet, so it contains nothing but Internet-style addresses.

In case you want to know when a sender cast a message into the void, the *Date:* line contains a timestamp of the event. The hapless driver in Figure 2.1 sent his message shortly before midnight on January 27, Eastern Standard Time.

▼

Reading Mail

Fresh messages end up in your mailbox as your system receives them. Mail-reading programs manipulate your mailbox and pull out individual messages at your command. Though its structure is simple, it is best to let the mail programs fiddle with your mailbox, rather than editing the file manually.

Mail readers use the headers of each message to determine where one ends and the next begins. Most importantly, the initial *From:* line is what delineates one message from the next. This is why if you send a message with *From* at the beginning of a line, it will arrive as *>From* so that the recipient's mail program doesn't think the text immediately following the embedded *From* is a new header.

UNIX has a number of ways of telling you that you have mail. As a normal part of the login procedure, UNIX will check to see if you have mail, and if you do, it will send a brief message to the screen. If you have an X Window interface into UNIX, you can use a little tool called **xbiff**, which is a tiny iconic mailbox that beeps and changes color when mail arrives. The UNIX shell will also periodically tell you when you have new mail by sending a brief *You have new mail* message to your screen. And, of course, there's the brute-force take-no-chances approach of simply invoking your favorite mail program and seeing if anything new has arrived.

When the recipient's computer receives a message, most of the header is already there. The computer adds the initial *From:* line and the receipt date, and then sticks the message in the recipient's mailbox. There, it waits for you to invoke a mail reader, which reads the mailbox file and offers various commands that you can use to manipulate the messages therein. The next chapter focuses on several mail commands, including **mail**, **mailx**, and **Mailx**.

This Chapter in Review

▲ E-mail and UNIX have been around since the 1970s.

▲ An e-mail address tells a computer (or network of computers) where to send a message, much as a postal address instructs the post office where to deliver a letter.

▲ On most systems featuring a graphical interface, the interface is set up to start automatically after you login the system.

▲ There are two primary forms of addressing: the Usenet form and the Internet form. The Internet form is much more common and simpler than Usenet.

▲ Converting between the Usenet and Internet forms is easy and may come in handy at times.

▲ When a computer receives e-mail, it puts it into a file called a mailbox. Each user has a mailbox, named after the user's login name.

▲ E-mail messages are composed of two parts: the header and the message body. The header contains information about how a message traveled to you, who it's from, and what it's about.

▲ A mail reader is a program that reads your mailbox and lets you manipulate your messages, as well as send e-mail to others.

▪ CHAPTER THREE ▪
Using Various UNIX Mail Tools

There are a number of UNIX mail readers in usage, ranging from the creaky old **mail** command to the more modern **mailx** command, as well as separately available freeware mailers like **elm** and **mh**. Topics in this chapter include:

- ▲ The command syntax for **mail**.
- ▲ The roots of the System V **mail** command.
- ▲ Reading and sending e-mail with **mail**.
- ▲ Comparing **Mail** and **mailx**.
- ▲ Using the **mailx** command.
- ▲ **Mailx** variables and tilde commands.
- ▲ Commands for sending and receiving mail with **mailx**.
- ▲ Customizing **mailx** with the **.mailrc** file.
- ▲ Using UNIX tools like redirection and **cat** to create mail.
- ▲ The Sun Microsystems Mail Tool.
- ▲ Using **elm** to read through your mail.
- ▲ A brief introduction to **mush**, **mh**, and *MIME.*

The Electronic In-Box

A lmost all UNIX systems feature electronic mail on some level. This mail can either be sent to other workers on your company or university UNIX system, or it can go to various other computer users who are tied at some level into the Internet. (When you send electronic mail out over the Internet, it doesn't matter if the recipient is using UNIX or another operating system.)

Like everything else in the UNIX world, different versions of UNIX feature different mail programs. The majority of UNIX users, however, use either the **mail** or **mailx** commands to send and receive mail.

This is not the forum in which to go into the different versions of UNIX, but suffice it to say that there are two primary strains of UNIX: System V and Berkeley. AT&T created System V, and the University of California at Berkeley created the Berkeley version, or BSD (short for Berkeley Software Distribution).

The version of **mail** included as part of System V UNIX works on mailbox files created by BSD UNIX, so compatibility isn't a problem. However, System V **mail** works a bit differently than **Mail**, BSD's mail reader. Just to confuse things a bit more, the **mailx** program found on some implementations of System V is virtually identical to BSD **Mail**. Since **mailx** is far more widely used than the BSD **Mail** command, this book will refer to **mailx** instead of BSD **Mail**.

Mail and **mail** are examples of UNIX commands. If you are unfamiliar with UNIX commands and how to use them, you might want to check out an earlier book in this series, such as *UNIX Basics*. (For instance, you should never forget that capitalization is important in UNIX, and that **Mail** and **mail** are actually two different commands.)

This chapter will cover the **mail** and **mailx** commands in some detail. In addition, other electronic-mail packages, such as **elm**, will be covered briefly at the end of this chapter.

Using System V Mail

One of the most common, and primitive, mail readers is the System V **mail** program.

You won't need to remember most of the details in this discussion. It's meant to explain how UNIX evolved and why there are several different ways to read mail in UNIX.

Since **mail** was one of the first mail readers, it lacks features found in more modern programs. The version of **mail** supplied on System V nowadays is a bit better than System 7 **mail**, but not by much. The following discussion focuses on System V **mail**, in all its crusty glory.

Reading your mail is easy—type **mail** at the UNIX prompt. If you have mail, the System V **mail** program will print the most recent message and then present you with the following prompt:

?

UNIX uses a number of prompts to indicate that the system is ready for input. If you're not familiar with prompts and their usages, consult *UNIX Basics* for more information.

▼

If you have no messages, **mail** will print a brief message, such as:

`No mail.`

As you can tell, UNIX is not known for its verbose error messages.

The **?** prompt is **mail**'s way of telling you it's waiting for a command. There are a number of commands available. The more important commands are listed in Table 3.1. In addition, Table 3.1 lists command-line options to the **mail** command.

TABLE 3.1 COMMAND REFERENCE FOR SYSTEM V MAIL PROGRAM

mail *options*

mail *options user*

mail *options user@address*

PURPOSE

The System V **mail** command reads your mailbox or sends a message or a file to a recipient at a local or remote location. When invoked without a recipient's address, mail will print the contents, if any, of a user's mailbox. When invoked with a recipient's address, **mail** will send a message or file to that recipient.

COMMANDS WHILE READING YOUR MAIL

Return key, +, **n**	Go to next message.
d or **dp**	Delete message and go on to next message.
d *num*	Delete message number *num*. Do not go on to next message.
dq	Delete message and quit mail.
h	Display a window of headers around current message.
h *num*	Display header of message number *num*.
h a	Display headers of all messages in your mailfile.

h d	Display headers of messages scheduled for deletion.
p	Print current message again.
-	Print previous message.
a	Print message that arrived during the mail session.
num	Print message number *num*.
r *users*	Reply to the sender and other *users*, then delete the message.
s *files*	Save message in the named *files* (**mbox** is default).
y	Same as **s**.
u *num*	Undelete message number num (default is last read).
w *files*	Save message, without its top-most header, in the named *files* (**mbox** is default).
m *persons*	Mail the message to the named *persons*.
q or **Ctrl-d**	Put undeleted mail back in the mail file and quit mail.
x	Put all mail back in the mailfile unchanged and exit.
!*command*	Escape to the shell to do *command*.
?	Print a command summary, a la help.
OPTIONS	
-ffile	**Mail** will use *file* for its mailbox instead of the default system mailbox.
-h	Header information is displayed rather than the latest message. The display followed by the ? prompt.
-p	Prints all messages.

▼

TABLE 3.1 CONTINUED

-q	**Mail** terminates after interrupts. Normally an interrupt causes only the termination of the message being printed.
-r	Messages are printed in first-in, first-out order, rather than the default of last-in first-out.
-t	Adds a *To:* line to be added to the letter, showing the intended recipients.

One of the more useful commands is **h**, which prints a one-line description for each message in your mailbox. Figure 3.1 shows some output from System V **mail** on a mailbox containing six messages, obtained by typing **h** and then **Enter** at the **?** prompt.

The **h** command is not available on all versions of UNIX.

```
6 letters found in /usr/mail/david, 5 scheduled for deletion,
0 newly arrived
    6   d   1776    eric@mastodon.CS.Ber  Sun Aug 14 12:44:19 1994
    5   r   1365    0003902103@mcimail.c  Fri Jul 22 22:42:11 1994
    4   s   12296   fusion@zorch.sf-bay.  Sat Jun 11 21:12:53 1994
    3   w   11227   fusion@zorch.sf-bay.  Thu May  5 05:12:35 1994
    2   y   786     molly!david@colossus  Sat Apr 16 10:52:07 1994
    >   1   2623    nobody@uunet.uu.net   Fri Apr 22 17:14:54 1994
?
```

FIGURE 3.1 A typical UNIX mail message

The number at the left of each line is the sequence number of the messages. The > at the far left indicates the current message. If you were to issue a command at the ? prompt that affected a specific message, the command would affect message number 1 in Figure 3.1.

The second number from the left is the size of the message in characters. Message number 6 is 1,776 bytes long. The next field is the address of the sender, followed by the date it was sent. Both of these fields are extracted from the header, while the size is derived from the message itself.

The addresses shown in Figure 3.1 are truncated after 20 characters. This is one of the drawbacks of the System V **mail** program. Also, **mail** sorts messages in reverse order of receipt. Message 1 is at the bottom of the list, while the most recent message, 5, is at the top. This is the default behavior for **mail**, though with some implementations of **mail** you can change it with the *-r* command-line option.

Most of the addresses shown are in the Internet format. This need not be the case if your mail gateway or the sender's gateway is not directly attached to the Internet. You might see some addresses with a few interspersed ! characters, as in message 2. On some implementations of System V **mail**, only the username portion of an address is shown.

Commands for Reading Mail

When you get e-mail, you will want to read it. When first invoked, **mail** will automatically print the most recent message received–6 in the example in Figure 3.1. After it prints the message to the screen, you will be presented with a ? prompt, at which you can enter any of a number of single-character commands. The ? command causes **mail** to print a list of these commands with a brief summary, in case you forget their subtle nuances.

After **mail** startles you with your most recent message, you can selectively read any message by typing its number and hitting **Enter**. One feature sorely lacking in System V **mail** is a paging program that prints one screenful of a message at a time (like UNIX's **more** or **page**). If you receive a lengthy message, it will fly by at a rate speed-reader Evelyn Wood would have difficulty keeping up with.

▲ **L E A R N   M O R E   A B O U T** ▲

There is a way to set up page-length displays of text within mailx, which you'll see later in this chapter.

The **p** command prints the current message; hitting **Enter** at the ? prompt will cause **mail** to print the next message. To back up and print the previous message, type a hyphen character (-), followed by the **Enter** key. You can step back through your messages by issuing successive hyphens.

In most of the messages in Figure 3.1, there is a letter between the message number and the size. This letter indicates what sort of operation has been performed on the message:

▲　　*d* indicates that the message has been deleted.

▲　　*r* indicates that the message has been read.

▲　　*s* indicates that the message has been saved to a file with its header intact.

▲　　*w* indicates that the message has been saved without its header.

▲　　*y* indicates that the message has been saved to a file with its header intact (*y* and s are identical in function).

In these latter three cases, once the message is saved it is slated for deletion.

The Good Aspects to System V mail

System V **mail** isn't totally brain damaged. It lets you repent if you've deleted a message that you don't want to delete.

You can undelete messages with the **u** command. When used without a message number, the current deleted message is recovered. Otherwise, the message number specified with the **u** command is undeleted.

To see which messages are on the chopping block, type:

h d

at the ? prompt. Other header commands are as follows.

▲ *h* displays a set of headers clustered around the current message.

▲ *h a* displays header information for all messages in your mailbox.

▲ *h #* displays header information for message number #.

In Figure 3.1, the first line indicates that five messages are scheduled for deletion. These are the five messages marked with letters *d, r, s, w,* and *y*. When you save a message in System V **mail**, it is automatically scheduled for deletion.

The first line in Figure 3.1 also indicates 0 newly arrived messages. If, during the course of reading your mail, new mail arrives, the banner line will change to indicate how many messages were put into your mailbox.

Two other important commands to know are **q** and **x**. Both exit from the **mail** program, but **q** updates your mailbox file first and then exits, whereas **x** exits without making any changes. If you deleted messages you really wanted to keep or aren't sure if you saved a message but have to leave the **mail** program, it is best to use **x** so that your mailbox is preserved in its original state, before you invoked **mail**.

Use the **x** command to leave System V **mail** if you are at all unsure about what you did to you mailbox. The **x** command preserves your mailbox in the state it was in before you invoked **mail**.

System V **mail** has a few command-line options, too. These are also summarized in Table 3.1. One (of many) annoying habit of System V **mail** is that it automatically prints the most recent message when you invoke it. You can prevent this behavior by using the *-h* command-line option:

```
$ mail -h
```

By using this option, you'll receive the list of one-line message descriptions, much like in Figure 3.1. You may find this far more convenient than getting blasted with your new messages from the get go. The antithesis of such patience is the *-p* option, which causes **mail** to spew the entire contents of your mailbox to the screen at once, without pausing at all. You might use this to dump your mailbox into another file.

Some versions of **mail** let you change the default sorting behavior from last-in first-out to first-in first-out order with the *-r* option. When invoked as:

```
mail -r
```

mail will appear with message 1, the first received, at the top of the message list rather than at the bottom, as in Figure 3.1.

The last notable option is *-f*, which instructs **mail** to use a file different from the default system mailbox as your mailbox. Say you've stored a number of messages from one particular person in a file called **boss**. You could type the following on the command line:

```
$ mail -h -f boss
```

and see a list of the messages you've saved. (Note the use of the *-h* option to prevent the latest-message screen-blast.) If you needed to look back over an earlier message, you'd simply instruct **mail** to print the desired message typing its number at **mail**'s ? prompt.

The other commands and command-line options listed in Table 3.1 are less commonly useful, but might come in handy at some point in your e-mail career. A few minutes' practice with each should be enough. You will probably most often find yourself using a few print and save commands, and leaving the more esoteric ones for daring experiments at two in the morning.

Casting Prose into the Void

E-mail would be pretty dull if all you could do was read mail sent to you. To truly seize the reigns of effortless global communication, you must send mail, too. Sending mail is easy. You need two things: the recipient's address and a message.

Let's say you wanted to send mail. To do so, you'd type the following command line:

```
mail kreichard@mcimail.com
```

and hit the **Return** key. Instead of the normal UNIX prompt, you will get a blank line. This indicates that **mail** is waiting for you to type in a message. Type in whatever text you want to send and hit **Return** at the end of every line. The **mail** program will not perform any fancy word-processing functions, so you'll have to format the text yourself. When your message is complete, type a period (.) alone on a line or **Ctrl-D**, and the message will be whisked away for delivery.

Unless your message is short, it is best to compose it first, store it in a file, and then mail this file to your addressee since System V **mail** lacks a decent editor in which to compose messages. It lets you make changes only to the current line of your message. Once you hit **Return**, you can't go back and change previous lines.

Your UNIX system features several text editors, including **ed** and **vi**. If you're not familiar with text editors, consult with your system administrator or the book *UNIX Basics*, also in this series.

You can send files to people by using the UNIX redirection operator. If you composed a message and stored it in a file called **message1**, you could e-mail that file by typing the following command line:

```
mail kreichard@mcimail.com < message1
```

The redirector (<) instructs UNIX to redirect the contents of **message1** into the **mail** program, which then sends it off. Another way to accomplish the same task is to pipe the contents of message1 into the **mail** program by typing the following command line:

```
cat message1 | mail kreichard@mcimail.com
```

▼

The pipe symbol (|) connects the output of one UNIX command into the input of another. In this case, you've piped the output of the **cat** command into the **mail** program, which will send the contents of **message1**.

As you can tell, redirection is an important aspect of UNIX usage. If you're not familiar with redirection, consult with your system administrator or the book *UNIX Basics*, also in this series.

When you use an editor to compose e-mail messages, make sure you save the message as plain ASCII text, not in a special word-processing format, like Microsoft *Word* or *WordPerfect*. E-mail transmissions do not handle binary characters well, such as are found in word-processing documents. If your message contains them, they probably will not make it to your recipient and might even cause your message to be lost altogether.

Another thing to watch for is exceedingly long lines. Some word processors put a carriage return or newline character only at the end of paragraphs, creating very long lines that can adversely affect mail programs. A likely result is that portions of the line that are too long will get truncated. It is best to put a newline character (**Return**) at the end of each screen line.

Once you send a message on its way, it is extremely unlikely that you can retrieve or cancel it. So be certain of a message before you cast it into the information sea. A letter composed and sent in anger can have irrevocable and costly consequences.

The Thoroughly Modern Mailx

With the discussion of the old System 7-derived **mail** program behind us, let's turn to a more modern mail-reading program that is shipped on most UNIX systems today: **mailx**. On some systems,

mailx goes by the name of **Mail**. For the most part—and definitely as far as you are concerned—the two are functionally very similarly.

 Note that **Mail** is spelled with a capital letter. UNIX is case-sensitive. Unlike DOS, UNIX distinguishes between uppercase and lowercase letters, so you must be careful and use the **Shift** key as necessary. Usually, mistakenly spelling something with a lowercase letter when it should have been capitalized won't do any harm—you just might be surprised by a different program than what you expected.

Mailx works with the same system mailbox as does **mail**, so you can use either to read your mail from the normal system mailbox.

Header Information

To read mail you simply type:

```
$ mailx
```

on the command line and the system will either respond with a list of one-line header descriptions for your messages, or it will print a message stating that you, alas, have no mail.

Figure 3.2 shows how **mailx** presents header information. You'll notice that it resembles the output of **mail** from the previous chapter, but that it is different in some ways.

 Note that the order of the messages is reversed, compared to System V **mail**. By default, **mailx** arranges messages in order of receipt: Earlier messages are at the top of the mailbox and messages received later accumulate at the bottom.

```
Mailx Tue Jun 22 10:41:18 PDT 1993 Type ? for help.
"/usr/spool/mail/david": 6 messages 3 new 6 unread
 U 1 paul@vix.com Fri Apr 8 17:14 59/2277 seen on bsdi-users mailin
 U 2 molly!david@colossus.apple.com Sat Apr 16 10:52 42/2225 chinese dinner
 U 3 fusion@zorch.sf-bay.org Thu May 5 05:12  243/11237 Fusion Digest 2428
>N 4 fusion@zorch.sf-bay.org Sat Jun 11 21:12 287/12296 Fusion Digest 2429
 N 5 0003902103@mcimail.com Fri Jul 22 22:42 37/1365 Where's chapter 4!
 N 6 eric@CS.Berkeley.EDU Sun Aug 14 12:44 51/1777 Re: thanks
?
```

FIGURE 3.2 Output from mailx

The > character points to the current message, as in System V **mail**. If you were to invoke a **mailx** command that assumed a message on which to operate, such as a save command, it would operate on the current message. The current message in Figure 3.2 is four.

The column of letters are codes indicating the status of the messages in the mailbox:

▲ *U* indicates that the message is unread.

▲ *N* indicates that the message is new.

▲ A blank space indicates that you've read the message.

▲ An asterisk (*) indicates that you have saved the message; after you save a message, it will be deleted from your mailbox when you exit **mailx**.

The message number follows the status code, and after it is the address of the sender. Unlike System V **mail**, **mailx** prints the entire address of the sender, not just the first 20 characters. The date the message was sent follows the address. Next comes some size information for the messages.

Mailx expresses a message's size with two numbers, separated by a slash (/) character. The first is the number lines in the message (in UNIX a line is a stream of characters terminated by a newline character, unlike in DOS, where lines are terminated by both carriage-return and line-feed characters). Following the slash is the number of characters in the message.

Last but not least is the subject of the message. If the message has a *Subject:* field, **mailx** prints its contents after the size information.

When you have dozens of messages in your mailbox, using the subject information can help you prioritize the order in which you read your mail. In Figure 3.2, every message has some subject information associated with it.

Reading Your Mail

With the contents of your mailbox summarized by the header information, you're now ready to manipulate your messages. You enter commands at **mailx**'s prompt; in Figure 3.2 this is the question-mark (?) character, but you can change it to anything you want (more on how to do this later). **Mailx** has all of the commands of System V mail and many, many more. Table 4.1 contains a command summary for **Mail**'s (numerous) commands. Fear not. All of them will not be discussed here.

TABLE 3.2 COMMAND REFERENCE FOR THE MAILX PROGRAM

mailx *options*

mailx *options user*

mailx *options user@address*

PURPOSE

The **mailx** program reads the contents of your system mailbox and displays the mail messages under your direction. When invoked with a recipient's address, whether a local or remote destination, **mailx** will send a message to that recipient. A message can be either a short note or a complete file. The commands below are helpful for reading mail that is in your mailbox.

COMMANDS WHILE READING MAIL

d *message(s)* delete *messages*	Deletes *message(s)* from your mailbox.
h *message* headers *message*	Prints the page of headers that includes the *message* specified, or the current message. The screen variable

TABLE 3.2 CONTINUED

	sets the number of headers per page. See also the **z** command.
? or help	Prints a summary of commands.
l or list	Prints all commands available. No explanation is given.
m *recipient(s)* **mail** *recipient(s)*	Mails a message to the specified *recipient(s)*.
p *message(s)* **print** *message(s)* **t** *message(s)*	Prints the specified *message(s)*. If the crt variable is set, messages longer than the number of lines it indicates are paged of lines it indicates are paged through the command specified by the PAGER variable.
exit or x	Exits from **mailx** without changing the system mailbox.
q or quit	Exits from **mailx** storing messages that were read in the **mbox** file (default) and unread messages in the system mailbox. Messages that have been explicitly saved in a file are deleted unless the variable KEEPSAVE is set.
r *message(s)* **reply** *message(s)* **respond** *message(s)* **replyall** *message(s)*	Replies to the specified *message(s)*, including all other recipients of that message. If the variable record is set to a filename, a copy of the reply is added to that file. If the replyall variable is set, the actions of **Reply/Respond** and **reply/respond** are reversed. The **replyall** command is not effected by the replyall variable, but always sends the reply to all recipients of the message.

R *message(s)* **Reply** *message(s)* **Respond** *message(s)* **replysender** *message(s)*	Sends a response to the author of each message in the *message(s)* list. The subject line is taken from the first message. If the variable record is set to a filename, a copy of the reply is added to that file. If the replyall variable is set, the actions of **Reply/Respond** and **reply/respond** are reversed. The **replysender** command is not affected by the replyall variable, but sends each reply only to the sender of each message.
***s** message(s) filename* **save** *message(s) filename*	Saves the specified messages in the named file. The file is created if it does not exist. If no filename is specified, the file named in the MBOX variable is used; **mbox** in your home directory is the default. Each saved message is deleted from the system mailbox when **mailx** terminates unless the keepsave variable is set. See also the **exit** and **quit** commands.
u *message(s)*	Restores deleted *message(s)*. This command only restores
undelete *message(s)*	messages deleted in the current mail session. If the AUTOPRINT variable is set, the last message restored is printed.
z[+][-]	Scrolls the header display forward (z+) or backward (z-) one screenful. The number of headers displayed is set by the screen variable.
!command	Escapes to the shell. The name of the shell to use is listed in the SHELL variable.

Probably the most common operations you will perform on your messages will be reading them and saving them. Typing a **p** at the **mailx** prompt will print the current message to the screen; if you want to summon a specific message, type **p** and the number of the message.

Similarly, typing **s** will save the current message into the default storage file, which is usually a file called **mbox** in your home directory. Alternatively, typing **s** *filename* will save the current message into a file called *filename*. As with the **p** command, you can specify a message number with the **s** command, too, and the specified message will be saved.

Getting even fancier, you can specify a range of messages to be saved. Typing **s1-4 flames** will save messages one through four into a file called **flames**. Multiple save operations to the same filename will result in the messages being concatenated together in that file; the file will not be overwritten by the latest message.

Two levels of helpful information are available within **mailx**. To get a list of **mailx** commands, type **?** at the prompt and a screenful of commands accompanied by brief descriptions will appear. This is useful for reminding you of the syntax for the various commands. Speed freaks can get a list of commands without any explanations by typing **l**.

As mentioned earlier, after you save a message, **mailx** slates it for deletion when you quit. You can explicitly delete a message with the **d** or **delete** command. Typing **d** alone will delete the current message, or you can specify a message number. You can delete a slew of message by specifying a range. For example, typing **d1-4** will delete messages one through four.

Unlike most of UNIX, **mailx** is forgiving: If you accidentally delete a message, you can undelete it with the **u** command. The **u** command also accepts message numbers as well as ranges of numbers, like **d** does. Successively typing the **u** command will undelete messages in reverse order of their deletion, that is, the last one deleted will be restored first.

There are two ways to get out of **mailx**—the **q** and **x** commands (you can use their full-word equivalents, too: **quit** and **exit**). As with System V **mail**, **q** will alter your mailbox as per the commands you issued during your session. Any messages you saved will be deleted from your mailbox and the status flags for messages left behind will be adjusted accordingly. The next time you read your mail, new messages will appear as unread messages and so forth.

The **x** command exits out of **mailx** without making any modifications to your mailbox. This is handy if you're unsure of what you've saved and deleted, and just want to back away slowly. Messages that arrive during your **mailx** session will be saved into your mailbox, but changes you've made will not be saved.

As with System V **mail**, the **x** command can be your salvation if you lose track of what you've done to your mailbox during a **mailx** session. It exits **mailx** without making any modifications to your mailbox.

After reading a message, you may want to send a note back to the sender.

The **r** command replies to just the sender of the message, while the **R** command replies to everyone who got the message as well as the sender. (Yes, the only difference is that one is a lowercase letter and one is an uppercase letter.) Typing enthusiasts can use the full-word equivalents for these commands: **reply** and **Reply**.

This is technical

Here, things get a little sticky between BSD **Mail** and System V **mailx**. In **mailx**, the **r** and **R** commands' functionality is reversed: **r** replies to everyone who got the message as well as the sender, and **R** replies to just the sender. Confusing? You bet. Now you know why people gripe about the different versions of UNIX. Subtle differences like these frustrate the living daylights out of innocents who must use different versions of UNIX.

As your popularity grows, you may find yourself with a mailbox chock full of messages. There may be so many, in fact, that the list of header information fills more than on screen.

Command

Not to worry. You can cope with this delirious state of affairs with the **z** command. Typing **z** advances you to the next screenful of messages; typing **z-** goes back to the previous screenful of messages. You can skip from screenful to screenful, perusing messages at will and reveling in your new-found electronic fame.

If you have a hankering to send a message to someone from within **mailx** and don't have a message from them to reply to, you can use the **m** or **mail** command. Typing:

m kreichard@mcimail.com

will invoke **mailx** and prepare to send a message. Sending mail with **mailx** will be covered below, but for now remember that you need not leave **mailx** to cast a message into the Void.

One fancy feature that **mailx** has and System V **mail** lacks is the shell-escape command. From within **mailx**, you can issue any UNIX command that you would ordinarily type at the command line. You can fire off UNIX commands by typing an exclamation point at **mailx**'s prompt and then the command you want to invoke. For example, if you want to get the current date and time from within **mailx**, you could type **!date** at the prompt and see the current system time printed. The shell-escape command is useful, too, for dropping down into a UNIX shell and fiddling about, then returning back into **mailx**. By typing **!csh**, **mailx** will invoke the UNIX C shell just as if you had logged into a new UNIX session. This can come in handy if you have to perform some quickie task but don't want to drop all the way out of **mailx** just to do it.

This is technical

It is inadvisable, though possible, to invoke **mailx** from within **mailx** with the shell-escape command.

Mailx's Command-Line Options

A list of **mailx**'s command-line options is in Table 4.2. Again, only a portion of this extensive list is worth covering. The rest can be left to late-night practice sessions or diversions during the work day.

TABLE 3.3 COMMAND-LINE ARGUMENTS FOR MAILX

USEFUL COMMAND-LINE ARGUMENTS	
-s *subject*	Sets the *Subject:* header field to *subject*.
-f *[filename]*	Reads messages from *filename* instead of system mailbox. If no filename is specified, the **mbox** is used.
-H	Prints summary of message headers only.
ESOTERIC COMMAND-LINE ARGUMENTS	
-e	Tests for presence of mail. If there is no mail, mail prints nothing and exits (with a successful return code).
-F	Records the outgoing message in a file named after the first recipient. It then overrides the record variable, if set.

▼

TABLE 3.3 CONTINUED

-i	Ignores interrupts (as with the IGNORE variable).
-n	Does not initialize from the system default **mailx.rc** file.
-N	Does not print initial header summary.
-u *user*	Reads *user*'s system mailbox. This is only effective if user's system mailbox is not read protected.
-U	Converts UUCP-style addresses to Internet standards. Overrides the CONV environment variable.

The three more useful command-line options are *-s*, *-f*, and *-H*. The *-s* option lets you specify a subject for an outgoing message on the command line, rather than waiting for **mailx** to prompt you. The syntax is simple. For example, typing:

```
$ mailx -s breakfast david
```

will prepare a message to the local user *david* with the subject *breakfast.* After you hit **Return**, **mailx** will wait for your input. You could also redirect a file into **mailx** using the < operator.

Subjects that are more than one word long can cause problems if you are not careful, as **mailx** considers the first word after the *-s* to be the subject. **Mailx** will interpret any following words as additional command-line options or recipients. You can include multiple words on command-line by enclosing the subject in double quotes. For example, typing:

```
$ mailx -s "breakfast meeting at 9:00" david
```

will set the subject to be *breakfast meeting at 9:00* for a message to *david*. The double quotes tell UNIX to consider what they enclose to be one word.

The *-f* option is similar to its System V counterpart. It lets you read mail from a mailbox other than then system default. Typing:

```
$ mailx -f mbox
```

▼

will read mail from the file **mbox**. This file must be a mailbox-style file and could be a series of messages stored by **mailx** itself. You may find it handy to store a series of related messages into one file, for easy retrieval later on. These messages might be from the same person, or they might pertain to a common subject.

When you invoke **mailx** with the *-H* option, it prints the one-line header information and exits. No changes are made to your mailbox. It is useful for seeing what your mailbox contains in one quick glance. **mailx** simply dumps this information to the screen, so if you want to save it you can redirect it into a file by typing:

```
$ mailx -H > filename
```

Alternatively, you can pipe the output through the UNIX **more** command:

```
$ mailx -H | more
```

Either approach is the kinder, gentler means to look at what might be multiple screenfuls of message headers.

Table 4.2 contains some of the more esoteric commands as well. Explore them at your leisure, for your pleasure. It is likely that you will never need to use them, but no UNIX command is complete without at least a dozen seemingly bizarre options.

Sending Mail with Mailx

The syntax for sending mail with **mailx** is much like System V **mail**. There are two crucial ingredients: a mail message and an address. The simplest form of a transmission would be:

```
$ mailx kreichard@mcimail.com
```

which would cause **mailx** to wait for you to type a message. (If configured appropriately, **mailx** will prompt you for a subject, but we'll cover that later on.) After your message is complete, issuing a **Ctrl-D** on a line by itself will send the message on its way. Alternatively, you can type:

```
$ mailx kreichard@mcimail.com < filename
```

where *filename* is a file that contains the message to be sent. **Mailx** is no more immune to non-ASCII characters than is System V **mail**, so be careful to send only ASCII files.

As with System V **mail**, **mailx**'s default editor is crude and permits you to make changes only to the current line. Once you type **Enter**, you can't alter the line unless you invoke one of **mailx**'s tilde commands. See Table 4.3 for a list of these commands.

TABLE 3.4 MAILX TILDE COMMANDS

~e	Invokes the editor to edit the message. The name of the editor is listed in the EDITOR variable.
~s *subject*	Sets the subject line to *subject*.
~c *name(s)*	Adds *name(s)* to the carbon-copy list.
~b *name(s)*	Adds *name(s)* to the blind carbon-copy list. This is like the carbon-copy list, except that the names in the blind carbon-copy list are not shown in the header of the mail message. (Carbon copy is referred to as *cc:*, while blind carbon copy is referred to as *bcc:*.)
~m *message(s)*	Inserts text from the specified *message(s)*, or the current message, into the letter. Valid only when sending a message while reading mail; the text the message is shifted to the right, and the string contained in the indentprefix variable is inserted as the leftmost characters of each line. If indent-prefix is not set, a tab character is inserted into each line.
~r *filename* ~< *filename* ~<! *shell-command*	Reads text from the specified *filename* or the output of the specified *shell-command*.
~! *shell-command*	Escapes to the shell. If present, run *shell-command*.

~?	Prints a summary of tilde escapes.
~v	Invokes a visual editor to edit the message. The name of the editor is listed in the VISUAL variable.
~l *shell-command*	Pipes the body of the message through the given shell-command. If shell-command returns a successful exit status, the output of the command replaces the message.

The tilde commands are a means to issue commands to **mailx** while in its crude default editor. Their format is simple. To call the visual editor (which is the best way to edit text), type ~v on a line by itself, and **mailx** will invoke whatever visual editor you have predefined, usually **vi** (more on how to tailor **mailx** to your whims later on). Alternately, you can use ~e to invoke the more obscure **ex** editor.

Some other tilde commands that you might find useful are ~s, ~c, ~b, ~m, and ~r. There are many more tilde commands, but these are the ones you'll likely use most often. The tedium of discussing the others is left as an exercise to eager readers.

The ~s command functions much like the -s command-line option, except with ~s you need not worry about enclosing multiple words within double quotes. Everything that you type after the ~s will become the mail message's subject line. You need not include a space after the ~s—just launch right into the subject of your choice.

The ~c and ~b commands perform similar functions, adding additional recipients to your mail message:

▲ ~c, for carbon copy, copies your message to other recipient and places their names in a *Cc*: field in the message's header.

▲ ~b, for blind carbon copy, copies your message to additional recipients, but does not make this fact known in the message's header.

Carbon copies are useful for routing material to a group of people that may have less of an interest in it than the primary recipient.

The ~**m** command can be used only when replying to a message. If you issue an **r** or **R** command from within **mailx** to reply to a message and then type ~**m** on a line by itself, it will incorporate the current message (the message to which you are replying) into your reply.

Typing ~**m num** will incorporate message number *num* into your outgoing message. If you have configured **mailx** appropriately (again, more on this later), a special character or set of characters is inserted at the beginning of each of the incorporated message's lines. See Figure 3.3 for an example. This is a common technique in e-mail and you will find yourself using it often. For example, you can incorporate a message into your reply and respond without having to rehash the sender's original text.

The standard character to begin the incorporated text's line is >, though you are free to tailor this to your own personal preferences. In Figure 3.3, you'll see several layers of embedded > sequences. These are from a message that contained an incorporated message and was then incorporated itself.

```
owen,

thanks for fixing the problem. it is a relief that all is
well with the world once more.

david

> Oops!!!
>
> You were right. Our DNS was a mass of agonies and screams.
> I fixed the cause of the trouble: an errant awk script.
>
> Owen
> > owen,
> >
> > realizing that for several hours now, all of our
> > incoming mail was being rejected because of a bizarre
> > problem, i decided to try a fix. i noticed that
> > /etc/advanced.hosts did not contain an entry for
```

```
> > uranium. i looked at /etc/hosts and saw that it was in
> > there and that its aliases had entries in
> > /etc/advanced.hosts but uranium did not. so, i added
> > uranium as an alias to itself, which seemed to fix
> > things. there must be a better fix. is a script going
> > haywire?
> >
> > david
```

FIGURE 3.3 Mail within mail

The final tilde command that deserves mentioning is **~r**, which incorporates a file into your message without prefacing its lines with any sort of additional characters. **~r** is useful for including a file into your message text.

Tailoring Mailx to Your Personal Tastes

It's time to discuss how you can customize the behavior of **mailx**. UNIX relies on several dot files to tailor its operation and the operation of some of its utilities to a user's desires. These files are called dot files because the filenames begin with a period (.). They don't appear in normal directory listings because **ls**, the UNIX directory command, is programmed to ignore them by default. You usually don't have to care that they're there once you've gone through the trouble of creating them anyway.

The dot file that customizes **mailx** is called **.mailrc**, which lives in your home directory. A sample **.mailrc** file is shown in Figure 3.4. It is composed of a series of one-line statements and definitions, each of which affects one aspect of **mailx**'s behavior. Table 4.4 summarizes some of the **.mailrc** statements. UNIX being what it is, there are, of course, many other esoteric variables that you can set. Explore these at the risk of a stroke by consulting your system's online-manual pages for **mailx**. (See the Appendix for more information on online-manual pages.)

TABLE 3.5 USEFUL .MAILRC VARIABLES

EDITOR=*shell-command*	Specifies the command to run when the **edit** or ~**e** command is used. Default is **ex**.
MBOX=*filename*	Lists the file that contains saved messages. The **exit** command overrides this variable, as does saving the message explicitly to another file. Default is the file **mbox** in your home directory.
PAGER=*shell-command*	Specifies the UNIX command filter for paginating output, along with any options to be used. Default is **more**.
SHELL=*shell-command*	Specifies a shell, if different than your default shell. Defaults to **/bin/sh**.
askcc	Prompt for the carbon-copy list after message is entered. Default is noaskcc.
asksub	Prompt for subject if it is not specified on the command line with the -s option. Enabled by default.
crt=*number*	Pipe messages having more than number lines through the command specified by the value of the PAGER variable (**more** by default). Disabled by default.
dot	Uses a single period at the end of a line to indicate that the message is completed.
hold	Preserve all messages that are read in the system mailbox instead of putting them in the standard **mbox** save file. Default is nohold.

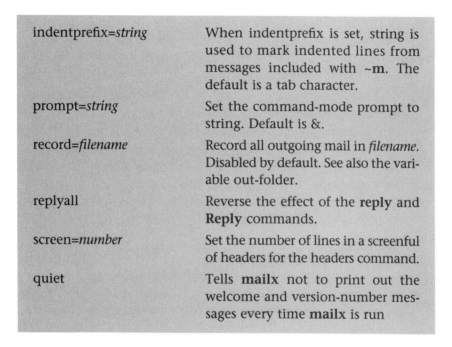

indentprefix=*string*	When indentprefix is set, string is used to mark indented lines from messages included with ~**m**. The default is a tab character.
prompt=*string*	Set the command-mode prompt to string. Default is &.
record=*filename*	Record all outgoing mail in *filename*. Disabled by default. See also the variable out-folder.
replyall	Reverse the effect of the **reply** and **Reply** commands.
screen=*number*	Set the number of lines in a screenful of headers for the headers command.
quiet	Tells **mailx** not to print out the welcome and version-number messages every time **mailx** is run

```
set EDITOR=/usr/bin/vi
set PAGER="cat -s | more -24 -c"
set SHELL=/bin/csh
set crt=24
set screen=20
set prompt='? '
set indentprefix='> '
set asksubj
set noaskcc
set hold
```

FIGURE 3.4 A sample .mailrc file

Let's run down the various lines in Figure 3.4's **.mailrc** file. You'll note that each line begins with the **set** command. In effect, the **.mailrc** file defines a slew of variables that **mailx** uses to determine how it behaves. The first line sets EDITOR, the editor to use when the ~**e** command is invoked. In this case, it is the full pathname of the **vi** text editor.

The PAGER line tells **mailx** how to deliver single screenfuls of a message. In Figure 3.4, a combination of UNIX **cat** and **more** commands is specified, although you could use any page-display command like **more** or **pg**.

Finally, the SHELL variable determines which shell program is run when ! commands are executed.

The crt variable sets the upper limit for the number of lines **mailx** will print to the screen. Messages that contain more than crt number of lines are put through the command specified by the PAGER variable to that they don't run off the screen in an eye-blink. The screen variable sets a similar criteria for the list of header information printed by **mailx**. Only the number of lines in the screen variable will be printed at a time.

The prompt variable sets the prompt that **mailx** uses to query you for commands. You can set it to anything you want. Spaces are preserved between single quotes. The indentprefix is the variable that specifies which characters, if any, are inserted at the beginning of an incorporated message's lines.

The next few lines do not require values. It is sufficient only to set them. They can be unset with by prepending *no* to the variable name. When set, the asksubj variable causes **mailx** to prompt you for a subject if you don't specify it with the *-s* command-line option. The askcc variable does the same thing for carbon copies. When set, it causes **mailx** to query you for additional recipients. When prefaced by *no*, as in Figure 3.4, **mailx** will not prompt for carbon copies of outgoing messages.

The hold variable, when set, instructs **mailx** to keep your messages in your system mailbox file until you explicitly save or delete them. Ordinarily, **mailx** will save messages that you've read into a file pointed to by the MBOX variable. The default is a file called **mbox** in your home directory.

That completes a small **.mailrc** file. You would do well to look at your system's **mailx man** pages to see the many other variables that aren't discussed here. You should find the ones in Table 4.4 suitable for most of your needs.

Mail Readers for Sun Microsystems Users

Not every major UNIX vendor relies on the **mail** and **mailx** commands for processing text. Some, such as Sun Microsystems, use graphical tools that send and receive mail. Though soon to be superseded by the Common Desktop Environment, Mail Tool from Sun's Solaris is still used by most Sun workstation users. As such, it's worth a mention.

Mail Tool does all of the things that have been outlined in this chapter. It will keep track of your incoming and outgoing mail messages, as well as informing you when new mail has been received. (An icon on the bottom of your screen indicates that a mail message has been received.)

To start Mail Tool, select **Mail Tool** from the **Programs** menu within the **Workspace** menu. The In Tray window will appear, containing a series of pulldown menus and a field for inputting a mail-file name. You'll also see a list of your mail messages (new and read), looking very similar to the list shown in Figure 3.2. To look at a mail message, double-click on the message line.

Sending a message is equally easy. The **Compose** button is your tool for starting a mail message. The buttons at the top of the screen— **Include**, **Deliver**, **Header**, **Clear**, and **Voice...** aren't really important for the most part; all you'll need to do is enter information in the *To:* and *Subject:* fields, as well as other recipients in the *Cc:* field if you want to send the message to other users. In addition, you can enclose a binary file with your mail message by clicking on the **File** button on the bottom of the screen.

Other Mail-Reading Programs

It's entirely possible that your UNIX system features another mail system. After all, the beauty of a UNIX system lies in the flexibility offered to system administrators and users.

And some vendors offer multiple electronic-mail options. Novell, for example, includes both a graphical mail-reading program and the **mailx** command. Various releases of SCO UNIX have featured varying mail tools.

The following are all popular UNIX mail packages. Because of space considerations, they can't be covered in the depth that the **mail** and **mailx** commands were covered. That doesn't mean that they are of lesser quality (usually the opposite, as a matter of fact)—it just means that they are used by fewer UNIX users than the built-in **mail** and **mailx** commands found on virtually every UNIX system.

Elm

Elm is a very handy mail program. Like **mail** and **mailx**, it keeps track of your incoming and outgoing mail messages. In addition, **elm** contains a number of features that are not found in the basic mail commands, such as the ability to automatically respond to other users when you go on vacation.

> ▲ **L E A R N   M O R E   A B O U T** ▲
>
> It is possible to forward messages as such with **mail** and **mailx**; it just takes a little more work than it does in **elm**. See Chapter 4 for more details.

The best thing about **elm**, however, is that it's incredibly simple to use, even for beginning UNIX users such as yourself. As you can see from Figure 3.5, **elm** gives you a lot of information about how to proceed when you go through your mail messages.

```
Mailbox is '/usr/mail/reichard' with 1 message [ELM 2.3]

N 1 Aug 13 Kevin Reichard (15) This is a test - only a test
N 2 Aug 14 Kevin Reichard (33) Proposed statement of purpose

You can use any of the following commands by pressing the first character;
d)elete or u)ndelete mail, m)ail a message, r)eply or f)orward mail, q)uit
```

```
To read a message, press <return>. j = move down, k = move up, ? = help
Command:
```

FIGURE 3.5 Elm in action

And that's about all there is to using **elm**. You can move between the messages with the cursor keys. As you can tell by Figure 3.5, you can enter the first letters of commands at the *Command:* prompt. (No obscure UNIX prompts here.)

The freeware **elm** program is not the same as the program named **Elm** found on versions of UNIX sold by Hewlett-Packard (HP-UX).

Elm can be found at many sites on the Internet. The handiest sites are archive sites for the *comp.sources.unix* newsgroup. At these sites (such as **ftp.cs.umn.edu**), you can find **elm** in the **/.archive1/usenet/comp.sources.unix/volume6** directory. In addition, there's a Usenet newsgroup devoted to **elm: comp.mail.elm**.

▲ L E A R N M O R E A B O U T ▲

You'll learn more about *archive sites* and *newsgroups* in Chapter 9.

Mush/Z-Mail

Mush is the *M*ail *U*ser's *SH*ell. When you run it, **mush** takes over the whole screen and also gives you many options for sending and receiving your electronic mail. In addition, **mush** contains a scripting language, used in situations where you're performing very similar actions.

You can get **mush** from any archive site for the *comp.sources.misc newsgroup*, including **usc.edu**, in the **/archive/usenet/sources/comp. sources.misc/vol32** directory.

> ## ▲ L E A R N   M O R E   A B O U T ▲
>
> You'll learn more about *archive sites* and *newsgroups* in Chapter 9.

An enhanced version of **mush** is sold commercially under the name **Z-Mail**.

Mh

Mh, for *Mail Handler*, integrates mail functions into the shell, rather than as a separate standalone program. While it offers advanced capabilities, it should also be used by intermediate or advanced UNIX users.

There is also a version of **mh** for the X Window System called **xmh**.

MIME

MIME is the hottest trend in the UNIX mail world. Standing for *Multi-Purpose Internet Mail Extensions*, *MIME* allows for internationalized messages and multimedia content, such as audio and video. You don't use *MIME* directly; rather, your mail program must support *MIME* (as does **elm**, for example).

This Chapter in Review

▲ System V **mail** is a primitive electronic-mail tool. Since many users are still stuck with it, **mail** is covered in this chapter.

▲ You use **mail** to send and receive your electronic-mail. **Mail** will save your electronic-mail messages to a file.

▲ The better mail tool is **mailx**, which ships with newer versions of UNIX. **Mailx** works on the same system mailbox as does System V **mail**, so you can use either one to read and send e-mail. **Mailx** offers a wealth of features, options, and nifty commands that System V **mail** lacks.

▲ As with System V **mail**, it is inadvisable to send binary characters with **mailx**. Make sure any messages and files you send contain only ASCII characters.

▲ The **.mailrc** file offers a means by which you can customize the behavior of **mailx**.

▲ Messages containing binary characters, as can be generated with word-processing programs, do not transmit reliably. Avoid including them in your e-mail messages. Extremely long lines in messages can cause problems, too. Limit each line to about a screen width and you'll do all right.

▲ Sun Microsystems workstation users can use the Mail Tool program for sending and receiving electronic mail.

▲ Other tools for UNIX mail include **mush**, **mh**, and **xmh**. In addition, the *MIME* extensions to mail programs allow video and audio to integrated into mail messages.

▪ CHAPTER FOUR ▪
Some Tips for Working with E-Mail

Now that you've learned the basics of sending e-mail with **mail** and **mailx**, it's time to put that knowledge into action by tackling a few advanced electronic-mail operations. Topics in this chapter include:

- ▲ Forwarding your mail to another address.
- ▲ The **.forward** file.
- ▲ Specifying multiple addresses in the **.forward** file.
- ▲ Filtering your forwarded mail.
- ▲ How to safely keep a copy of incoming messages for yourself.
- ▲ Forwarding mail to a group of people.
- ▲ Telling people you're on vacation with the **vacation** command.
- ▲ Why you should avoid the **sendmail** program.
- ▲ Privacy and electronic mail.

Teaching New Dogs Old Tricks

The previous chapter covered the basic command structures of the **mail** and **mailx** commands. As such, you were exposed to only the most basic of operations—mainly, sending and receiving electronic mail.

This chapter goes a step beyond and tells you how to make advantage of these commands, as well as some other UNIX mail-related commands.

Forwarding Mail

Mailx has the ability to easily forward incoming e-mail automatically to another address, which you might want to do if you go away on a business trip or take a vacation and desperately need to read your e-mail.

A simple way to forward your mail is to use the *-F* option to the **mailx** command. With it, you merely specify the place to forward your mail. You can add the following line to your existing mailbox file (usually **mbox** in your home directory, unless you have changed it:

```
Forward to kreichard@msit.edu
```

Or you can use the *-F* option to **mailx**:

```
$ mailx -F kreichard@msit.edu
```

When you want to turn off the mail forwarding, use the following command line:

```
$ mailx -F " "
```

In addition, you can use other files and scripts to forward your mail in a more elaborate manner. You remember the **.mailrc** file from the previous chapter. It, along with other dot files, configure various UNIX programs for operation in your user environment. In addition to the **.mailrc** file, **mailx** also uses the **.forward** file. This file doesn't need to exist. In fact, it's best to create this file only when you want your incoming mail to be routed somewhere else besides the standard system mailbox. Like the **.mailrc** file, **.forward** lives in your home directory.

The format of the **.forward** file is very simple. If you wanted all of your incoming mail to be routed to another destination, you would simply put the address for that new destination in your **.forward** file. Once the file was saved, all incoming mail would arrive and then get sent by the system to the new address. The address can be either a local user address or a remote e-mail address. It doesn't matter.

For example, say you were on sabbatical in South Haven, Minnesota, doing some postgraduate work at the Minnesota State Institute of Technology. While you were away, you'd want all of your e-mail forwarded to your university mailbox. To do this, simply put your university address in your **.forward** file:

```
kreichard@msit.edu
```

This address will cause the mail system to send incoming mail back out to the Minnesota State Institute of Technology. When it arrives at its final destination, you can use the UNIX mail-reader of your choice to read and respond to messages just as if you were back home. The e-mail header will contain some additional hops that might not otherwise exist, but the message will be the same. Voila! Instant change of address. And the best thing is, the sender won't know you've changed locations because your old address works just fine.

There's no such school as the Minnesota State Institute of Technology. Don't bother sending electronic mail to the above address.

Once you return from faraway lands, simply delete the **.forward** file and your incoming e-mail will be dumped into the system mailbox.

If you want to forward mail to more than one address, you can put multiple addresses in the **.forward** file. Just make sure they're all on one line separated by commas. For example, say you wanted to keep a copy of your mail in your standard system mailbox, but also pass on a copy to an account you have at another location. You could put this line in your **.forward** file:

```
\kevin, kreichard@msit.edu
```

▼

Once in place, this line will cause mail to be dumped in your local system mailbox as well as sent out to your account at the Minnesota State Institute of Technology. The backslash (\) character before your name is necessary to tell the system not to continue processing the incoming message. If it weren't there, a message would arrive, the system would check your **.forward** file and see that it should forward the message to local user david and the remote address. It would then deliver the message to user david and encounter the **.forward** file all over again, and try to deliver it to david again (and again, and again, and again...). The backslash prevents this sort of nasty infinite loop from occurring.

Having two addresses in your **.forward** file can come in handy if you have a system at home that you want a copy of your incoming mail sent to. If you work at home on occasion and you don't want to worry about missing out on e-mail traffic, you can automatically forward a copy of your correspondence to your home office. This requires, of course, that you have an e-mail system at home and a link between it and whatever means you need to deliver mail, such as the Internet.

Care should be taken when putting an address in the **.forward** file. If you make a typo or the address is simply bogus, your e-mail could very well be lost for good. A typo of a local user's address might be caught by the local system doing the processing. But if the address is for a remote location, it's possible that the next stop for your incoming e-mail will be oblivion.

Mail-Handling Scripts

In addition to e-mail addresses, you can also put the names of programs in the **.forward** file—programs that are designed to handle e-mail in some way. For example, say you go on vacation and instead of having your mail pile up in the system mailbox, you want it placed into separate files. If you had a program that accepted incoming e-mail messages and deposited them into a file named after their senders, you could specify the location of this program in the **.forward** file:

```
|/home/kevin/bin/mh
```

▼

When a message arrives, the mail system would pipe it into the **mh** program, whose complete pathname you specified in the **.forward** file. After this point, it's **mh**'s responsibility to take care of the message. The pipe (|) character at the beginning indicates that **mh** is a program, rather than some bizarre form of e-mail address. (See the previous chapter for a short explanation of the **mh** program.) If, for whatever reason, your mail-handling program requires arguments, you must enclose the entire program string and its arguments in double quotes:

```
"|/home/kevin/bin/sortm fishing."
```

In this case, the argument *fishing.* might specify the prefix for the filenames that **mh** creates out of each incoming message.

Take care when writing mail-handling programs. Test them out before you put an entry in your **.forward** file. An easy way to test your program is to **cat** a mail message (that you've saved into a file) through your program and check to make sure it did what it was supposed to do. For example, say that **fusion.1** is a file that contains a message from the Fusion Digest mailing list and **mh** is a shell script that dumps each day's feed into a separate file. If you were to do:

```
cat fusion.1 | /home/david/bin/mh
```

the **mh** program should process the incoming data stream as if it had arrived via e-mail and place the message into the daily Fusion Digest file. You would also want to test that **mh** puts non-Fusion Digest messages into your mailbox.

Figure 4.1 contains a simplified version of the **mh** program described above. Such scripts can get complicated quickly and before you customize the one shown, bone up on Bourne shell so that you know precisely what is going on and how to armor the script against failure.

```
1   ## Mail-handling script to catch Fusion Digest mailing list feed.
2   ## Incoming messages not from Fusion Digest are dumped into the system
3   ## mailbox.
4   ##################################################################
5
6   MBOX=/var/spool/mail/david
7   ERR=/home/david/.mh.err
```

```
 8   TMP=/home/david/.mh$$
 9   umask 077
10
11   ##
12   ## Define a function to dump incoming mail into mailbox.
13   ##############################
14   dump_to_mbox ()
15       n=`(grep -n '^$' $TMP | line | cut -d":" -f1) 2> /dev/null`
16       if [ ! -f $MBOX -a ! -w `dirname $MBOX` ]
17       then
18           echo "`date`: mh: cannot write to $MBOX" >> $ERR
19       else
20           sed -e "$n:=0,s/^From/>From/" $TMP >> $MBOX
21           echo "" >> $MBOX
22       fi
23
24
25   ##
26   ## Define a function to clean up files.
27   ##############################
28   clean_up ()
29       if [ -f $TMP ]
30       then
31           /bin/rm -f $TMP
32       fi
33
34
35   ##
36   ## Dump incoming mail message into a temporary file.
37   ##############################
38   cat - > $TMP
39
40   ##
41   ## scan for Fusion Digest marker in Subject: field.
42   ##############################
43   G=`(grep "^Subject:[   ]*Fusion Digest" $TMP | line) 2> /dev/null`
44
45   if [ "$G" ]
46   then
```

```
47      FILE=/home/david/delphi/fusion/`date +%j`
48      cat $TMP >> $FILE
49      clean_up
50      exit
51  fi
52
53  ##
54  ## No matches; dump to mbox and clean up.
55  #############################
56  dump_to_mbox
57  clean_up
```

**FIGURE 4.1 A sample mail-handling script
to process feeds from the Fusion Digest**

The first four lines are comment lines that describe what the script does. Never underestimate the value of comments and use them liberally. Lines 6, 7, and 8 set some important variables that are used elsewhere in the script. MBOX is the full pathname for the system mailbox, ERR is the name of the file that will contain **mh**'s error output (perish the thought), and TMP is the name of the temporary file that will hold the incoming mail message while **mh** is processing it.

Lines 14 through 23 define a function that dumps the contents of TMP into the system mailbox. One of the things you'll notice in some of the messages you receive is that a > character has been placed before any occurrence of *From* that falls at the beginning of a line. This is to prevent mail readers, such as **Mail**, from thinking that a new message begins at the *From*. By having your mail-handling script put messages in your system mailbox instead of the e-mail system, you'll have to put a > character in front of any initial *From* lines. This is what the **sed** line in dump_to_mbox does. Buried within its crypto-syntax is the vital conversion from *From'* to *>From* (it wouldn't hurt to study the **man** page for **sed** to see what the other parts of this line do). Note the use of the >> operator rather than >. This ensures that incoming messages will be tacked onto the end of the system mailbox, instead of over-writing earlier messages.

Lines 28 through 33 set up a garbage-collector function. Line 38 is a simply cat invocation that redirects the incoming mail stream into the file specified by TMP. Lines 43 through 51 are the guts of **mh**. They check to see if the incoming mail message is from the Fusion Digest mailing list. It accomplishes this by seeing if a particular string exists in the subject field of the message. Mail from Fusion Digest always contains *Fusion Digest* as part of the subject string, so the script uses **grep** to detect its presence. If a hit occurs, the message, now contained within the temporary file, is copied onto the day's *Fusion Digest* file, specified by the FILE variable. The *date +%j* command tacks on the numerical day of the year to the full pathname for this file. It is always best to specify complete pathnames within mail-handling scripts to be certain that things get dumped where you want them.

If *Fusion Digest* is not found in the message's subject field, the message is copied into the system mailbox specified by the MBOX variable and the program cleans up after itself by removing the temporary file.

Always verify that you mail-handling scripts work as you want them to before you create a **.forward** file to invoke them. You can cause the loss of your incoming e-mail if there is a mistake—no matter how small—in your script. Checking scripts is easy: just pipe some test messages through them and see if they behave as they should. Get help from your system administrator if you run into problems.

There is plenty of opportunity to add scans for other incoming messages. If you wanted to divert mail from a particular user, you could scan the *From* lines of messages and check for the username of interest, manipulating it as you see fit. This is an easy way to get rid of junk e-mail if you're getting pestered by annoying persons out in the Void.

When configuring mail-handling scripts to detect mail from specific sources, be certain that the string you're scanning for uniquely describes that source. For instance, note that in Figure 4.1, only the subject line is searched for the occurrence of *Fusion Digest* rather than the entire message. It is conceivable that a message could contain this string and not be from the Fusion Digest mailing list. Limiting the search to just the subject line decreases the likelihood of the script mistakenly diverting a message into the fusion files. It is true that a message might have the string in its subject line and might not be from the list, but this is a far rarer eventuality.

The paranoid among you may feel uneasy handing over control of all your incoming e-mail to a shell script. To ensure that a copy of your mail always gets put into your system mailbox, use a **.forward** file like this:

```
\kevin, |/home/kevin/bin/mh
```

This file instructs the mail system to put incoming messages into the system mailbox, as well as pipe them through a mail-handling script. If the script drops the ball and sends e-mail to an untimely demise, the message will be safe and sound, cooling its heels in the mailbox. Until you're certain your script works, it is best to use this sort of insurance against catastrophe.

Forwarding Mail to a Group

You may also want to forward all mail to a group. You can do this directly from the command line, using the aforementioned *-F* option:

```
$ mail -F "johnsone@camax.com,reichard@mr.net"
```

Gone Fishing

Custom mail-handling scripts are one way to process incoming e-mail, but what if you don't want to spend hours debugging voodoo shell scripts and simply want to announce to the outside world that you will be away from your desk for a few days? The UNIX **vacation** program may be your ticket to freedom. It performs a straightforward service: Once properly set up, it will respond to incoming e-mail with a message written by you, usually specifying how long you will be away from your e-mail. It automatically sends this message to whoever sends you e-mail.

The **vacation** program is invoked much as mail-handling programs are, with an appropriate entry in your **.forward** file:

```
\kevin, "|/usr/bin/vacation kevin"
```

Note the use of double quotes around the command string. This is so **vacation**'s command-line argument (*kevin* in this case) is passed to the program. Also note the backslash (character before *david*, which prevents pesky infinite loops during mail processing. It is always best to specify the full pathname of the **vacation** program, which could vary from system to system. Before using **vacation**, obtain its correct full path and put it in your **.forward** file.

The message that **vacation** sends out is stored in the file **.vacation.msg** in your home directory, where your other dot files are kept. You can either edit this file before hand, or invoke **vacation** from the command line and interactively create this file. You may find it simpler to create the file first, place the entry in your **.forward** file, turn out the lights, and go on your merry way.

Some versions of **vacation** have a default message that can be used. Here is one version:

```
From: kevin (via the vacation program)
Subject: Gone Fishing

I will not be reading my mail for a while, as I am fishing
in the mountains of Montana. Your mail regarding "$SUBJECT"
will be read when I return.
```

Note the *From:* and *Subject:* lines telling recipients who this message is from and its import. Also note the *$SUBJECT* string in the body of the message. When **vacation** sends this message out, it will replace this string with the contents of the incoming message's subject field. This is a handy feature to let the recipient know which message was received by the **vacation** program.

Rather than repeatedly replying to each and every sender of mail to you, **vacation** will wait a default of one week before sending the **vacation** message to any given sender. It keeps a record of folks to whom it's sent mail in two database files—**.vacation.pag** and **.vacation.dir**—in your home directory. The **vacation** program consults these files when an e-mail arrives for you. If no entry is found for a sender, **vacation** sends out the **.vacation.msg** message and puts an appropriate entry in the database files. If the sender sends another message within the

▼

default of one week, **vacation** does not respond. If, however, a week elapses, and you are still away, **vacation** will once again send your missive into the Void.

There are a few command-line options for **vacation**. These are summarized in Table 4.1. The *-I* option (on some systems this may be a lowercase *-i*) causes **vacation** to initialize the database file **.vacation.pag** and **.vacation.dir**. This is recommended each time you configure **vacation** to respond to incoming mail. It is best to start with a clean slate. The *-I* option is the only one for human use on the command line. The other options should be placed in the invocation string within your **.forward** file.

TABLE 4.1 COMMAND REFERENCE FOR THE VACATION PROGRAM

vacation *options*

vacation *options user*

PURPOSE

The **vacation** command automatically responds in your absence to incoming e-mail messages. It sends out a predefined message to each sender and waits a specified period of time before responding again to that sender.

COMMAND-LINE OPTION

-I	Initialize the **.vacation.pag** and **.vacation.dir** files and start **vacation**.

OPTIONS FOR USE WITHIN THE .FORWARD FILE

-a *alias*	Indicate that alias is one of the valid aliases for the user running **vacation**. Mail addressed to that alias generates a reply.
-j	Do not check whether the recipient appears in the *To:* or the *Cc:* line.

TABLE 4.1 CONTINUED

-t*N*	Change the interval between repeat replies to the same sender. The default is one week. A trailing *s*, *m*, *h*, *d*, or *w* scales *N* to seconds, minutes, hours, days, or weeks, respectively (not available on all systems).

On some systems, notably those from Sun Microsystems and its clones, the *-j* option causes **vacation** to respond blindly to every sender of e-mail to you in your absence. It will not check to see if you actually appear in the *To:* or *Cc:* fields of the e-mail message. You might think that you would always appear in these fields if the message is being delivered to you. Normally, you would appear, but if you are part of a system alias (more on these later), your username would not necessarily be in the header. If you want to have **vacation** send its message to every incoming mail message, use this **.forward** file (substituting your own name, of course):

```
\kevin, "|/usr/bin/vacation -j kevin"
```

The *-a* option allows you to list alternate names to which incoming e-mail could be addressed. This is sort of a selective form of the *-j* option above. You can specify aliases of which you might be a part and to which you want **vacation** to send its message. For example, use this **.forward** file to send **vacation** messages in response to mail from the fusion alias:

```
\kevin, "|/usr/bin/vacation -a fusion kevin"
```

Some systems let you alter the default waiting period of one week that **vacation** abides before sending out repeat messages. The SunOS version of **vacation** has the *-t* option, which provides a fine degree of control over the waiting period. Using *-t2w* changes the period to two weeks; *-t3s* changes it to three seconds (not recommended). Other units of time permitted are minutes (m), hours (h), and days (d). This invocation will cause **vacation** to wait only one day before sending repeat **vacation** messages:

```
\kevin, "|/usr/ucb/vacation -t1d kevin"
```

Systems lacking the *-t* option may use a *-r* flag, followed by a number, which alters the waiting period to that many days. Other **vacation** implementations lack the ability to change the waiting period entirely. Welcome to the variable world of UNIX.

Do remember to either remove your **.forward** file or replace it with a non-**vacation** one when you return. Otherwise, **vacation** might continue to announce to the outside world that you are away when you may, in fact, be toiling at your desk.

The Horrors of Sendmail

As your use of UNIX grows, you will see your system administrator be possessed of a variety of moods. The foulest of these emotional states will probably be when something is going wrong with a seemingly innocent utility called **sendmail**. It is best to approach the administration staff with caution during these episodes.

The **sendmail** program is the e-mail workhorse of many UNIX systems. It was written by Eric Allman at Berkeley several years ago and revised over the years to become commonplace in machines from many different vendors. You will likely never use **sendmail** directly. It is not designed to be used by humans, but rather serves as an intermediary between the outside world and your mailbox. When you finish composing a message and type a **Ctrl-D**, it gets handed off to **sendmail** for delivery. If the recipient is local, **sendmail** arranges for the message to be delivered to the local mailbox. If the recipient is on a different machine than you, **sendmail** connects to a network, possibly the Internet, and hands the message to an instance of **sendmail** running on the remote machine. The final delivery of the message now rests in the hands of the remote system.

Two files control how **sendmail** behaves: **sendmail.cf** and **aliases**. The **sendmail.cf** file is the configuration file, and it contains a few system-specific definitions and a set of rules that **sendmail** uses to interpret a mail message's address. These rules are so inscrutable as to drive normal innocents insane. You should never attempt to fiddle with your **sendmail.cf** file. Pay somebody to make adjustments for you so that you have someone to sue when something goes wrong. The role of **sendmail** on your UNIX system is vital, but its configuration and administration can bring even erudite gurus to their knees.

Sendmail is mentioned here only to warn you against making any changes to its crucial and fragile **sendmail.cf** configuration file. The other file, **aliases** (usually contained in **/etc/aliases**) is safe to play with and comes in quite handy at times. As its name suggests, it contains a list of **aliases**, or alternate names for users at your site. There can be one **aliases** file per system, which **sendmail** consults during the processing of e-mail messages.

The format of the **aliases** file is simple. The alias comes first, then a colon, and finally the list of addresses that will be mapped to the alias. For example, say you want to establish a list of folks in your office that all can be referenced by the name managers. The appropriate line in the **aliases** file might be:

```
managers : huey, dewey, louie
```

Whenever you make changes to the **aliases** file you must run a program called **newaliases**, which processes the file so that **sendmail** can see the changes.

If the members of an alias are numerous, you may find it convenient to use multiple lines by beginning each follow-on line with a tab character. For example, this:

```
managers : huey, dewey, louie
```

is identical in function to:

```
managers : huey, dewey
<TAB>louie
```

Once this alias is established, you can send mail to managers and **sendmail** will process it and deliver it to huey, dewey, and louie. Alias file entries are good for mapping common misspellings to a person's username. For example, these entries:

```
dburnett : david
dburnette : david
dave : david
burnett : david
burnette : david
```

will cause the various spelling permutations to point to an actual user-name, which is *david* in the example.

You can do fancy things with the **aliases** file as well, such as map an alias to a program. Just as your **.forward** file can direct incoming mail into a mail-handling script, an **aliases** entry can do the same. Say you have some fax software on your system. You could put an entry in your **aliases** file to pipe mail going to a fax alias into the fax software:

```
fax : "|/usr/local/bin/faxtransmit"
```

Your fax software might use a phone number included in the subject field of the message and report an error if it cannot find one.

The **newaliases** program will report any errors it finds, as well as duplicate aliases. It also provides some statistics. Here is some sample output:

```
/etc/aliases: 359 aliases, longest 148 bytes, 9068 bytes total
```

You normally won't care about this data, unless it is not what you would expect. For instance, if you have an enormous **aliases** file and **newaliases** reports only three aliases, something might be going wrong.

Aliases established in the **aliases** file work for e-mail coming in from the outside world as well as messages sent locally. The fax alias shown above is dangerous in that it would permit people at other sites to send faxes on your dime just by sending mail to *fax@spacely.com* (if you worked for Spacely Sprockets).

Aliases can refer to other aliases. For example, this entry:

```
staff : managers, ducks
ducks : donald, mickey
managers : huey, dewey, louie
```

▼

sets up staff as an alias that points to ducks and managers. Mail sent to staff will get delivered to donald, mickey, and huey, duey, and luey.

Note that staff comes before ducks and managers in the file. This is okay. The **newaliases** program will sort out the definitions just fine.

Usually, the ability to edit the **aliases** file is a privileged operation and requires root access. If you do not have root access and wish to create **aliases**, contact your administration staff. The kindly souls should be glad to set up an alias for you.

Privacy

There is ongoing debate about the legal status of e-mail. Businesses are free to establish their own policies with regard to the privacy of e-mail on their computer systems. It is best to check with your administration staff to find out your company's policy on e-mail privacy and other security issues. Some organizations consider e-mail to be as strongly protected as postal mail from prying eyes. Others consider it to be the property of the institution owning the computer systems (and remember that these are the people who—for the moment—have the law on their side.)

Most folks would feel violated if they found out that someone else was reading their mail and incensed if they learned that someone was sending false transmissions under their name. If you suspect that someone is snooping your mailbox, report it to your administration staff or whoever you think is appropriate.

It is difficult to determine if your mailbox has been read by someone other than you, but suspicious changes, such as messages getting deleted in unknown ways or your mail-reading program reporting errors or detecting garbage in your mailbox, could be signs of tampering.

Though your system mailbox is probably kept in a public place, its permission bits are usually such that only you have read and write access. You may want to periodically check to be sure that all is well by issuing a command like this:

```
ls -l /var/spool/mail/david
```

Which yields:

```
-rw---- 1 david users  90232 Jul 27 01:08 /var/spool/mail/david
```

Note the solitary *rw*. This is how it should be. One sign of tampering may be that the group and world permission fields are also set. If they are, contact your administrator.

Once you save e-mail messages into files, they are susceptible to snooping as well. You can give yourself a modicum of protection by setting the UNIX file permission bits to grant only read access to you and no one else. However, if a snooper has root privileges, you are basically doomed as any file can be read (or deleted) by such fiends. A corrupt superuser is an evil thing in UNIX land.

Some versions of UNIX offer basic encryption utilities that you can use to encrypt saved messages. See if your system has the **crypt** program and, if so, read the **man** page to see how it's used.

There are some commercial and public-domain packages as well. If you border on the paranoid and want to have this added level of security, contact your administration staff to see what they can offer. You may want to ask about the freeware PGP package (short for Pretty Good Privacy). It is considered to be fairly secure and offers a variety of encryption features for e-mail communication.

▼

This Chapter in Review

▲ The **.forward** file lets you easily forward mail to other addresses.

▲ In addition to forwarding mail elsewhere, the **.forward** file can preserve a copy of mail in your system mailbox.

▲ Further adding to the power of the **.forward** file, you can specify the name of a program or script that will process incoming mail in elaborate ways.

▲ When deploying any mail-handling script, make sure it works correctly before you put an entry into your **.forward** file that invokes it.

▲ The **.forward** file is used to invoke the **vacation** program.

▲ The **vacation** program permits you to inform people sending you e-mail that you may be out of touch for a period of time.

▲ The **sendmail** utility should be handled with care.

▲ The **aliases** file can be very useful for establishing aliases for groups of people or for channeling mail into special-purpose programs.

▲ Privacy is an important aspect of e-mail. Find out your company's policy on e-mail privacy.

▲ Be wary of system snoopers reading or altering your mailbox.

▪ CHAPTER FIVE ▪
Working with UUCP

The UUCP program provides an easy way to transfer files between UNIX systems. It hails from the early days of UNIX, but lives on as a hearty workhorse suitable for moving files over modem lines. Topics in this chapter include:

- ▲ UUCP's configuration files.
- ▲ The all-important **Systems** file.
- ▲ How to copy files from one system to another.
- ▲ UUCP's useful command-line options.
- ▲ **uuname** and **uulog**.
- ▲ Welcome to the machine—a snippet of a UUCP logfile.
- ▲ Some sources of potential problems with UUCP transfers.
- ▲ Sending mail with UUCP.

▼

Introducing UUCP

In the old days of UNIX when the Internet was the information highway of a privileged few academic researchers, UUCP served as a means to link together thousands of UNIX machines in a loose association known as Usenet, distributing electronic mail and newsgroups to tens of thousands of users. (It is this network that saw the widespread use of the Usenet style of e-mail addresses discussed in Chapter 2.)

However, UUCP enjoyed a wider usage than merely tying into the Usenet. Many corporations use UUCP to transfer data between machines in different locations over phone lines on an ad-hoc basis. And even now some sites use UUCP to download mail packets from a remote system that's directly connected to the Internet. In short, UUCP can be used to transfer information from one UNIX machine to another UNIX machine.

There's a certain amount of confusion surrounding UUCP. For starters, UUCP usually refers to both a set of programs that facilitate UNIX-to-UNIX communications and a program that goes by the name of **uucp**. For the purposes of this chapter, UUCP refers to the suite of programs in a general sense, and **uucp** refers to the specific program.

Several versions of UUCP (short for UNIX-to-UNIX copy program) have appeared over the years, culminating in **HoneyDanBer** (an amalgam of its three creators: Peter **Honey**man, David A. Nowitz, and Brian E. **Redman**) UUCP, considered by some to be the easiest to use (though this might not be saying much). This chapter will cover the ins and outs of HoneyDanBer UUCP, since this is the version in common use today. You'll find UUCP to be part of most UNIX implementations. If you have a modem connected to your machine and have other sites to which you have access, you can make use of UUCP.

This is technical!

There are actually several different versions of UUCP floating around. However, the HoneyDanBer version is the most common (at times, system documentation will refer to the HoneyDanBear version in less colorful terms—Basic Networking Utilities, or BNU), and so

▼

this chapter will concern itself mainly with this version. If you find that the instructions in this chapter don't work with your system, check with your system administrator; it could be that your system features a different version of UUCP.

What does UUCP do? Simply put, it is a means by which you can transfer a file from one computer to another over the phone. You can either send files or retrieve files, or both. A benefit of UUCP is that it provides error correction during the transmission, so if the phone line is noisy, UUCP can recover any missing data.

Another nice thing about UUCP is that you can send binary files, or files that contain non-ASCII characters. Remember how some e-mail systems recoil in horror from binary files? UUCP is no slouch in this regard and cares not whether the file is pure, golden ASCII or harbors 8-bit binary characters.

Though UUCP is used most often over dial-up modem lines, it can also be used to move files between systems over any connection, be it a network, parallel line, or direct-wired serial cable. Other file-transfer utilities are better suited to, say, network environments, but UUCP does see some use in hard-wired serial connections between local machines. For instance, you could have two PCs running UNIX and sharing mail and files over a serial-line UUCP link. Though crude, this sort of set-up provided a basic form of networking before the wide-spread use of PC LANs and Ethernet.

This is technical

UUCP is merely the human interface into what amounts to a suite of utilities that UNIX uses to transfer files between systems. The actual program that does the communicating is **uucico**. An instance of **uucico** running on your system will connect (through a modem, say) to an instance running on the remote machine. The two programs negotiate the line speed, handle the error checking, and do all the nifty things that makes UUCP a handy tool to have.

This chapter covers the basics of UUCP, including file transfers and electronic mail. The next chapter covers the Usenet, while Chapter 7 focuses on other UUCP commands that allow you to link directly to other systems, including the **cu** and **uux** commands.

▼

Configuration Files

Several configuration files are necessary for UUCP to function properly. Four files in particular are crucial for UUCP operation: **Systems**, **Permissions**, **Dialers**, and **Devices**. They are usually found together in one place, which can vary from UNIX to UNIX. Some common locations are **/etc/uucp** or **/usr/lib/uucp**. It is probably best to have your administrator fiddle with these files, but a background knowledge of their role in UUCP's functioning will help you understand how UUCP works.

The **Systems** file contains a list of the machines, one per line, to which your machine can attempt a connection. In addition to the remote machine name, there is the phone number, modem speed, and chat script that your machine will use to log into the remote system. Figure 5.1 contains a few lines from a **Systems** file. The lines beginning with the # character are comment lines and are ignored by UUCP. They are useful for embedding helpful information, such as the format for the important lines toward the end of the file. The last two lines are the connection data for two remote machines, **beast** and **trillian**. You can see their machine names in the first field.

```
# Entries have this format:
#
#  Machine-Name Time Type Class Phone Login
#
# Machine-Name node name of the remote machine
# Time day-of-week and time-of-day when you may call
# (e.g., MoTuTh0800-1700). Use "Any" for any day.
# Use "Never" for machines that poll you, but that
# you never call directly.
# Type device type
# Class transfer speed
# Phone phone number (for autodialers) or token (for
# data switches)
# Login login sequence is composed of fields and subfields
# in the format "[expect send] ...". The expect field
# may have subfields in the format "expect[-send-expect]".
```

```
#
beast Never ACU 9600 5919720 "" \d\r in:-in: nuucp word: binstock
trillian Any ACU 19200 8261531 "" \d\r in:-in: nuucp word: macarthy
```

FIGURE 5.1 A portion of a UUCP Systems file

The second field is the time during which connections can be placed. This is *Any* in the *trillian* line, which means calls can be placed at any time of day. More restrictive time slots can be specified, all the way down to *Never*, which means that outgoing calls can never be placed, but rather the remote machine would have to dial your system.

The next three fields are the device to use (specified by a code, which translates into an entry in the **Devices** file), the communication speed to use for the connection, and the phone number to dial.

The last portion is the chat script, which consists of a series of receive/send pairs separated by spaces. The pair of double quotes in the figure specifies that UUCP should wait for nothing before sending a delay (\d) and then a carriage return (\r). The next element tells UUCP to wait for an *in:* string, which is the tail end of a *login*: prompt common to most UNIX systems. When this string is detected, UUCP will send the login name—**nuucp** in both examples—and then wait for the *password:* prompt, to which it will respond with the passwords listed (don't bother attempting to connect to these systems, as the telephone numbers and passwords are bogus).

If you have a system you want to access via UUCP, your administrator can help you set up the connection now that you know what information UUCP needs.

The **Permissions** file attempts to control the level of UUCP access to and from other sites. Entries specify which directories can be read or written to, and offer a means to verify the authenticity of the remote system. The **Devices** and **Dialers** files are nasty little creations that tell UUCP which modems to use (based on the device code in the

Systems file) and how to control the modems. Whenever you get close to hardware in UNIX, things take a gruesome turn, and the **Dialers** file is no exception. Leave its configuration in the faithful hands of your administrator.

Using UUCP

With the foundation for UUCP laid, it's time to explore the use of the specific **uucp** program, which is surprisingly simple given the complex underpinnings of the program. The syntax for **uucp** is akin to **cp**, the UNIX copy program, which is probably no coincidence.

Table 5.1 contains a command summary for **uucp**.

TABLE 5.1 COMMAND REFERENCE FOR THE UUCP COMMAND

uucp *options local_file remote_system!remote_file*

uucp *options remote_system!remote_file local_file*

PURPOSE

The **uucp** command copies files between UNIX systems connected by a modem or serial line.

OPTIONS

-c Uses the source file when copying out rather than copying the file to the **uucp** spool directory. This is the default.

-C Makes a copy of outgoing files in the **uucp** spool directory, rather than copying the source file directly to the target system. This lets you remove the source file after issuing the **uucp** command.

-m Sends mail to the requester when the file transfer is complete.

-r Do not begin the file transfer right away—just queue the job.

For example, you wanted to copy the file **book.txt** from your system to *trillian*. You would use this command:

```
$ uucp book.txt trillian!/usr/spool/uucppublic/book.txt
```

The machine names listed in this chapter, such as *trillian*, are fictional examples. Don't bother using these machine names in any practice sessions.

Note the rather elaborate destination-file specification. The directory **usr/spool/uucppublic** is the usual directory into which files are copied. If you wanted to copy **book.txt** to any other directory, chances are you would run into permissions problems. Most systems tend to batten down the hatches fairly tightly when it comes to **uucp** and file transfers in general, so don't expect to be able to gallivant all around a remote system just because you're using **uucp**. Many restrictions are likely to exist, but you can assume that the **uucppublic** directory is a safe haven.

The *trillian!* portion of the command line tells **uucp** which remote system to copy **book.txt** to. The address style is very much Usenet (remember the multiple exclamation points used in a typical Usenet mail address?), which is no surprise given the ancestry of **uucp**.

Users of the C shell must follow a slightly different procedure for specifying the name of the system. If you've worked with the C shell at all, you know that the exclamation mark (!) has a slightly different meaning—it refers to the C shell's *history* capabilities. In order for the C shell to properly process a command like:

```
# uucp book.txt trillian!/usr/spool/uucppublic/book.txt
```

you'll need to tell the C shell that the explanation mark applies to the name of the system and not to the C-shell syntax. Do so by placing a backslash before the exclamation point:

```
# uucp book.txt trillian\!/usr/spool/uucppublic/book.txt
```

You could use this method in any shell, actually, since the Bourne shell won't choke on the backslash (to the Bourne shell, the backslash is irrelevant).

Most systems do not pass along **uucp** requests, so hops through multiple machines probably won't be possible. Don't expect a command like this to succeed:

```
$ uucp book.txt uunet!trillian!/usr/spool/uucppublic/book.txt
```

It is likely machine *uunet* will not honor the **uucp** request.

> ### ▲ L E A R N   M O R E   A B O U T ▲
>
> On the other hand, requests made by the **mail** program via a UUCP connection are usually honored. See "Sending Mail with UUCP" later in this chapter.

You can pluck files from remote machines using **uucp**, provided you have the necessary permissions to do so. Say that **book.txt** is in *trillian's* **/usr/spool/uucppublic** directory. This **uucp** command issued from *molly* would copy **book.txt** to *molly's* **uucppublic** directory:

```
$ uucp trillian!/usr/spool/uucppublic/book.txt molly!/usr/spool/uucppublic
```

You could also use this slightly abbreviated form:

```
$ uucp trillian!/usr/spool/uucppublic/book.txt /usr/spool/uucppublic
```

 Since you initiated the **uucp** command from *molly*, it assumes that the destination for the file copy is also *molly*. Note also the lack of an explicit destination filename. If none is given, **uucp** will assume you want to use the same name as the source file.

When **uucp** is invoked, it spools your request in a spool directory tucked somewhere safe in your system files. Some common ones are:

```
/usr/spool/uucp/machine_name
```

- or -

```
/var/spool/uucp/machine_name
```

where *machine_name* is the name of the remote system. Depending on how your system is set up, your machine might attempt to establish a connection immediately, or wait until the appropriate time to call. Most UNIX systems that maintain UUCP connections have a daemon that periodically checks for spooled **uucp** requests and, if it finds any, will begin the file transfer. Again, this scheduling is nothing you have to worry about; setting a policy in this matter is a job for the system administrator.

Several command-line options alter the behavior of **uucp** and are listed in Table 5.1. For transfers from local to remote systems, **uucp** does not ordinarily copy the file to its spool directory, but rather reads the file from whatever directory it happened to be in when the command was executed (i.e., as if the *-c* option were used). To cause **uucp** to make a copy of the local file in its spool directory, use the *-C* option. This way, you are free to delete the local file and **uucp** won't complain about not finding it when the transfer is attempted. Using the *-c* option permits **uucp** to work faster, as it doesn't have to make a copy of the local file, while avoiding unnecessarily filling up the spool directory. Sometimes the spool directory may not have enough available space to copy the local file, in which case **uucp** will fail.

If you want a receipt to be mailed to you when a file transfer is completed, use the *-m* option. If you were to type this command:

```
$ uucp -m book.txt trillian!/usr/spool/uucppublic
```

uucp would send you an e-mail message reporting that the transfer occurred (assuming the operation was successful).

Ordinarily, **uucp** would try to initiate a file transfer as soon as you type the command. The *-r* option prevents this from occurring and causes **uucp** to queue your request, which will get executed whenever your system regularly dials out. A command like this causes **uucp** to wait for the system daemon to initiate the connection:

```
$ uucp -r book.txt trillian!/usr/spool/uucppublic
```

Other UUCP Goodies

Two other commands complement UUCP: **uuname** and **uulog**.

The **uuname** command simply prints a list of the machines to which your system can establish UUCP connections. Here is some output from a well-connected machine in California:

```
$ uuname
beast
trillian
basis
portal
ucbvax
mtxinu
wl
```

Do not confuse **uuname** with **uname**.

Assuming everything is properly configured, you theoretically could transfer files to and from any of these systems from the machine **uuname** was executed on. The **Systems** file is the source for **uuname**'s information, so any system **uuname** returns must also have a **Systems** entry.

The **uuname** command is summarized in Table 5.2.

TABLE 5.2 COMMAND REFERENCE FOR THE UUNAME COMMAND

uuname *options*

PURPOSE

The **uuname** command lists the UNIX system that can be accessed with UNIX communications tools like **mailx** or **uucp**.

OPTIONS

-c   Prints system names that can be accessed with the **cu** com-
      mand. (Not available on all systems.)

-l   Prints the name of the local system.

The **uucp** program maintains a logfile of its activities, which can be very useful if connection problems arise (it seems that UUCP is a particular favorite of Murphy). The uulog command prints out the contents of this logfile. Table 5.3 contains a brief reference for **uulog**'s two command-line options.

TABLE 5.3 COMMAND REFERENCE FOR THE UULOG COMMAND

uulog *options*

PURPOSE

Uulog prints the contents of the **uucp** logfile. Its various options limit the output to specific systems or provide a continuous update of the logfile.

OPTIONS

-s*system*   Prints information about connections involving the
              specified *system*.

-f*system*   Does a **tail -f** of the file-transfer log for **system**. You
              must initiate an interrupt to exit this function.

The *-ssystem* option instructs **uulog** to limit its output to the specified system. Without specifying a remote system, **uulog** will print the contents of all its logfiles, one for each remote system with which the local machine maintains UUCP connections. To get the log output for machine *trillian*, this command would suffice:

```
$ uulog -strillian
```

▼

If you want to monitor the progress of a connection and any file transfers that (you hope) take place, use the *-fsystem* option. The new entries to the logfile for the specified system are printed continuously, as if a **tail -f** command had been performed on the file.

> ## ▲ L E A R N   M O R E   A B O U T ▲
>
> **Tail** which prints the tail end of a file, is a UNIX command that falls outside of the para-meters of this book. See *UNIX Basics*, the first book in the UNIX Fundamentals series, for more information on the **tail** command.

The command:

```
$ uulog -ftrillian
```

would provide a continuous report of UUCP's interaction with machine *trillian*. The language used in the file is a little arcane at first, but with experience you should be able to sift out key words, like *ACCESS DENIED* if a file could not be collected from or written to a remote system.

Figure 5.2 contains a excerpt from a logfile on machine *molly* for connections to *trillian*. The *REMOTE REQUESTED* lines are files downloaded from *trillian* to *molly*, and the *REQUEST* line indicates that a file was uploaded to *trillian*.

Note the timestamp buried in the string of numbers enclosed within parentheses.

```
uucp trillian (8/1-23:44:46,19423,0) SUCCEEDED (call to trillian )
uucp trillian (8/1-23:44:51,19423,0) OK (startup)
uucp trillian (8/1-23:44:54,19423,0) REMOTE REQUESTED
 (trillian!D.tril18570d75- > molly!D.tril18570d75 (daemon))
```

```
uucp trillian (8/1-23:45:47,19423,1) REMOTE REQUESTED
(trillian!D.molly8619f08- > molly!X.trilliaN8570 (daemon))
uucp trillian (8/1-23:45:49,19423,2) REMOTE REQUESTED
(trillian!D.trill8571813- > molly!D.trill8571813 (daemon))
uucp trillian (8/1-23:45:52,19423,3) REMOTE REQUESTED
(trillian!D.molly861a813- > molly!X.trilliaN8571 (daemon))
david trillian trilliaN6a04 (8/1-23:45:53,19423,4) REQUEST
(molly!/tmp/.s19436- > trillian!/home/david/molly/mis/07.pgp
(david))
uucp trillian (8/1-23:45:57,19423,5) OK (conversation complete ty00
116)
```

FIGURE 5.2 Excerpt from a uulog report for machine trillian

Sending Mail with UUCP

On a more mundane level, you can use UUCP to send mail between connected systems. (Remember, the entire point of Usenet electronic-mail addresses—as explained in Chapter 2—is to send mail via a UUCP connection.) To do this, simply summon the **mail** command and then specify a machine to connect to:

```
$ mail trillian!kevin
```

This command would send mail to *kevin* on the machine named *trillian*, assuming that your UNIX system has a UUCP link to *trillian*.

With this command, you could also compose the mail message. After hitting the **Return** key after the command line, you can just go ahead and type your mail message:

```
$ mail trillian!kevin
Kevin:
This is an example of a mail message sent over UUCP.
—Geisha
```

When you hit the **Return** key within the mail message, you're only telling **mail** to begin the next line of the mail message. To end your mail message and send the mail on its way, hit **Ctrl-D**.

As you learned in Chapter 3, you can also use UNIX redirection to specify a file as input for a mail message, as in the following:

```
$ mail trillian!kevin < note
```

This would use the file named *note* as the body of the mail message.

Reality Check: Problems with UUCP

If you experience problems transferring files, take a peek at the logfile for the ornery system in question and consult your administrator if there are any error messages. Many things can go wrong with UUCP requests:

▲ If the connection occurs over a dial-up line, the modem at the other end could be busy. Or the modem could have simply failed and died. Remember, no hardware device is guaranteed to work 100 percent of the time—at least no modem is, anyway.

▲ Generally speaking, mail requests sent with UUCP are not instantaneous, unless there's a direct connection between machines. If your system relies on a modem link to another machine, you're at the mercy of whatever schedule your system administrator uses. Some system administrators queue UUCP requests and send them out every so often, such as once an hour. Many other system administrators queue all the UUCP requests to the late-night hours, when phone rates are cheap and UUCP requests are made to a distant machine.

▲ If your system is having difficulty logging into the remote system, chances are that a password or login has changed and you were not informed. This happens all the time, especially for systems set up to automatically change passwords every so often.

▲ If your system does successfully log into the remote machine, but **uucp** reports access-denied errors, check the pathnames for the files involved. Often it's a matter of a simple typo.

▼

Sites tend to restrict UUCP's access fairly severely, so it's likely you simply can't read or write to the file (or directory) you want. It's best to send files to the **/usr/spool/uucppublic** directory, as this is usually writeable by everyone.

This Chapter in Review

▲ The UUCP set of commands and programs is an easy way to move files and electronic mail between UNIX systems.

▲ It's easy to confuse UUCP (the suite of commands) and **uucp** (one of the suite of commands. Be sure you can tell the difference in this chapter.

▲ The syntax of the **uucp** command is very reminiscent of the UNIX **cp** command.

▲ Several configuration files—including **Systems**, **Permissions**, **Dialers**, and **Devices**—determine which systems **uucp** can communicate with, and how it controls the modems available to it.

▲ **Uuname** provides a list of machines to which yours has access.

▲ **Uulog** provides a means to examine the UUCP logfiles, which can come in handy if problems occur.

▲ You can also send electronic mail via a UUCP connection, using the Usenet-style of electronic-mail addressing discussed throughout this book.

▲ A variety of things can go wrong with a **uucp** connection, ranging from the mundane (modem busy), to the pesky (password change at remote end).

Madge soaks her
nails before getting
on Usenet.

▪ CHAPTER SIX ▪
The Usenet

The Usenet can be viewed as the world's largest exchange of information between computer users. When approached correctly, the Usenet can be a valuable source of information, especially information about computing itself. Topics in this chapter include:

- ▲ Usenet newsgroups: An overview.
- ▲ Separating the good newsgroups from the bad.
- ▲ Typical Usenet articles.
- ▲ Using **rn** to read the news.
- ▲ Using **nn** to read the news.
- ▲ Posting articles with **pnews** and **Postnews**.
- ▲ Some guidelines when postings articles.
- ▲ Using Frequently Asked Questions, or FAQs.
- ▲ Drawbacks to the Usenet.

93
▼

A Leaky Umbrella Term

When people speak of the Internet or the 'Net, they tend to lump together every electronic offering—electronic mail, Usenet newsgroups, and the World Wide Web. Yet the reality of the situation is that not every UNIX user has total access to every electronic offering of the 'Net. Many users have access to only one or two aspects of the 'Net.

It also takes many different tools to access the various offerings of the 'Net. For instance, the popular *NCSA Mosaic* is an Internet *browser*, meant for cruising between hyperlinked documents. You can't use *NCSA Mosaic* to read through the Usenet newsgroups, nor can you use *NCSA Mosaic* to read and send electronic mail. As you've learned time and time again in your UNIX education, the UNIX operating system breaks down tasks into small, manageable chunks—and that philosophy extends to UNIX connections to the electronic world.

In the last chapter, you learned about the UUCP commands and how they can be used to send electronic mail and files between interconnected systems. This chapter extends the discussion of UUCP with an overview of the Usenet, which also relies on UUCP capabilities to send information back and forth between UNIX systems. Your system administrator will make sure that you have a feed from the Usenet; your role is to read the news.

 Don't confuse the Usenet newsgroups with the **news** command. The **news** command is used to read news sent by your system administrator only to users of your UNIX system.

What is Usenet?

The Usenet (short for **User's Net**work) is also an umbrella term, but generally speaking it refers to a collection of computers that pass along *newsgroups:* open discussions devoted to various topics of interest to the computer world. These discussions range from the ridiculous (**alt.barney.dinosaur.die.die.die** and **alt.sex.bestiality.barney**) to the sublime (**alt.beer**). As of this writing, there were over 5,000 Usenet newsgroups. Some, such as the aforementioned Barney groups, are on the fringe, while others, such as discussions relating to UNIX and other computing topics, are much more credible in their contributions to society.

The name of a newsgroup follows a very precise pattern, beginning with the general category, followed by the precise topics of the group. When we look at a newsgroup named **alt.barney.dinosaur.die.die.die**, we can see that the name begins with a category of *alt*, which is Usenet shorthand for an alternative newsgroup. There are many newsgroup categories; the major ones are listed in Table 6.1.

TABLE 6.1 MAJOR USENET NEWSGROUP CATEGORIES

CATEGORY	SUBJECT
alt	Alternative topics, ranging from sex (**alt.sex. bondage**) to Barney the Dinosaur to super-models (**alt.supermodels**) to beer (**alt.beer**). These newsgroups tend to come and go quickly; it takes a small group to request the creation of an **alt** newsgroup, and when interest in the groups wane, they are quickly dropped.
bionet	Scientific topics, centering on biological information.
biz	Business topics, where companies are allowed to blatantly advertise their wares; not exactly the best source of unbiased information, unless you have a technical questions about a specific product.
comp	Computing, ranging from groups for beginners to advanced discussions of computer science.
gnu	Discussions of products from the Free Software Foundation, creators of such popular UNIX tools as **emacs** and **gcc**, the GNU C compiler.

TABLE 6.1 CONTINUED

k12	Discussions for schools, ranging from kindergarten to senior high. (Obviously, the kindergarten teachers will be more interested than the students in these newsgroups.)
misc	Rooms that don't fit under any other subject area.
rec	Recreational topics, ranging from the music of the Grateful Dead and REM to crafts and beermaking.
sci	Scientific topics apart from computer science. A big favorite in the academic world.
soc	Social topics, such as mating rituals or ethnic groups.
talk	The Usenet equivalent of talk radio, with the requisite emphasis on politics and religion.

In addition to the newsgroups categories listed here, there are other minor categories devoted to corporations (such as *dec*, short for Digital Equipment Corp., a large player in the UNIX world) and regions or countries (for instance, **mn.general** is a general newsgroup for Minnesota-based Usenet users, while newsgroups beginning with *ba* are meant for the San Francisco Bay Area).

As mentioned earlier, there are currently over 5,000 Usenet newsgroups. Some, like **alt.barney.dinosaur.die.die.die** or **mn.general**, are of interest to only a small group of Usenet users. Others, such as **comp.unix.questions**, are of interest to a larger group of Usenet users—there are probably many more people interesting in learning more about the UNIX operating system than those wanting to see Barney the Dinosaur die. (In fact, **comp.unix.questions** is a good newsgroup for you to read, since it's meant for UNIX beginners. **Alt.barney.dinosaur.die.die.die**, on the other hand....) To obtain a list of newsgroups, you should first subscribe to the newsgroup called **news.lists**, which periodically lists all of the worldwide (that is, newsgroups not of local interest) newsgroups. (Some newsgroups are listed in Appendix B.) You could also consult one of the 107 books devoted to the Internet.

Unless you're working for a large company with a ton of computer disk space devoted to a Usenet feed, your system administrator probably hasn't subscribed to every Usenet group. (A feed is merely Usenet news sent as one big chunk.) Getting a feed from every newsgroup takes of a *lot* of disk space, and it's not uncommon for a newsfeed to "blow out" (or overwhelm) a computer's storage system—after all, a typical Usenet feed will run between 20 megabytes and 40 megabytes *per day*.

The structure of a Usenet newsgroup is unique, but easy to grasp once you've read through it. When someone contributes to a newsgroup, they are said to *post* news. When you read through a newsgroup, you can read the posts—known formally as *articles*—in the order they were posted, or (if your software allows it) you can read through a thread of posts—articles that are posted in response to one another. A thread is simply an ongoing discussion of a specific topic. Depending on your software, you can respond to the post by sending your response to the entire newsgroup (where it becomes part of the ongoing thread), or you can respond directly to the poster via electronic mail. A formal standalone Usenet post is shown in Figure 6.1, while an informal post that's part of an ongoing thread is shown in Figure 6.2.

```
From: dwex@aib.com (David E. Wexelblat)
Subject: XFree86[TM] 3.1 Progress Report...
Date: 25 Aug 1994 12:48:59 -0700
Keywords: XFree86, 3.1

                  XFree86[TM] 3.1 Status Report
                  -------------------------------

Release currently planned for mid-to-late September, 1994.

Major Features:
    - X11R6-based, including shared libraries for SVR4, Linux,
      FreeBSD and NetBSD.
    - XIE, PEX, and LBX supported.
    - HiColor (15/16-bit) support for Mach32 and S3 servers.
    - HiColor (15/16-bit) and TrueColor (32-bit) for P9000 server.
```

32-bit color means 24-bit color aligned on 32-bit boundaries.
Modes with 24-bit packed pixels are not supported.

New hardware support:
- Weitek P9000 server, preliminary testing for Diamond Viper
  [VLB/PCI, and Orchid P9000 boards.
- IIT AGX server. Preliminary testing for AGX-014, AGX-015, and
  AGX-016 chipsets, with a variety of RAMDACs.
- S3 864/964 support in S3 server. Preliminary testing for just
  about every board we could locate that uses one or the other.
- Support for S3 GENDAC clock/RAMDAC.
- Western Digital WD90C33 support, including acceleration.
- Cirrus 5434 accelerated support.
- SVGA driver for MX68000/MX68010
- SVGA driver for AL2101
- SVGA driver for Cirrus CL6420
- SVGA driver for Video7
- New ATI SVGA driver

FIGURE 6.1 A typical Usenet announcement, presented here in partial form

From: ab574@freenet.carleton.ca (Brett Mackey)
Subject: Re: Red Cap Ale (I've tried it)
Date: 24 Aug 1994 14:10:52 GMT

In article <1994Aug21.130617.1@nickel.laurentian.ca>,
g1400014@nickel.laurentian.ca wrote:

> Hello folks,
>
> Has anyone tried the rereleased Red Cap ale yet?
>
> It is my understanding that Brick or someone licenced it from the
> original brewer.
>
> Cheers
> Carlo

Yes, Brick does brew the beer and it's rather unremarkable. It does
prove a point though. That microbreweries can imitate commercial
beers but why they would want to is another matter.

--

ab574@freenet.carleton.ca

FIGURE 6.2 A typical Usenet posting to the alt.beer newsgroup

In the case of Figure 6.1, the leader of the XFree86 development
group, David Wexelblat (*dwex@aib.com*), was reporting to the computer
community at large about the progress of XFree86 (*Subject:
XFree86[TM] 3.1 Progress Report...*), a freely distributed version of the X
Window System for PC-based Unices. His comment appeared in the
comp.x.announce newsgroup. In Figure 6.2, a Canadian user was
commenting on beer. (No surprise there, eh?)

How do you know that it was a Canadian user? Because the user's
address ends in *ca*. Countries aside from the United States
(remember, America is the center of the universe) usually add a
country suffix to an electronic-mail address: *ca* for Canada, *uk* for
Great Britain, *jp* for Japan, and so on.

In order for everyone to keep track of the different pieces of information in the thread, it's considered good form to quote the post
you're responding to. In Figure 6.2, this practice is shown in the
following text:

```
Subject: Re: Red Cap Ale (I've tried it)
...
In article <1994Aug21.130617.1@nickel.laurentian.ca>,
g1400014@nickel.laurentian.ca wrote:

> Hello folks,
>
> Has anyone tried the rereleased Red Cap ale yet?
>
> It is my understanding that Brick or someone licenced it from the
```

```
> original brewer.
>
> Cheers
> Carlo
```

Here, we see the subject of the article (since the subject is in reference to another article—hence the *Re:*—we know it's a response) and a portion of the original article. Most UNIX newsreaders automatically quote the previous article after you decide to respond to it

▲ **L E A R N   M O R E   A B O U T** ▲

You will learn more on that process during discussions of the specific newsreaders.

And most UNIX newsreaders structure the previous post by listing the name of the original poster and number of the previous post, followed by the text of the previous post preceded by > symbols.

Generally speaking, it's good to quote *only* the portion of the article that you're responding to. When you respond, your software will automatically quote the entire text of the preceding article. You're free to delete some of the quoted text as you shape your response.

A Usenet newsgroup is structured in two different ways. Most newsgroups allow anyone to post information and respond to other posts, as shown in both Figures 6.1 and 6.2. For instance, anyone can post their favorite method of killing Barney the Dinosaur in **alt.barney.dinosaur.die.die.die**. These groups are ruthlessly egalitarian: You must wade through the meanderings of crackpots (see "Drawbacks to the Usenet," later in this chapter) to get at the true nuggets of information. Some more useful newsgroups—usually of a more narrow focus and technical or scientific in nature—are *moderated*. Here, you send your post to a moderator, who then decides whether to pass your contribution to the rest of the Usenet.

Usenet Conventions

As you use the Usenet more and more, you'll see that conversing on the Usenet has evolved into its own little language. While this language and lingo may seem to deter the participation of newcomers (and, indeed, it's used by the more snobbish users of the Usenet for precisely this purpose), don't let it bother you. You'll soon find that many of the obscure acronyms on the Usenet actually serve a purpose, as a kind of shorthand for commonly used phrases. Some of the more common acronyms are listed in Table 6.2.

TABLE 6.2 SOME COMMON USENET ACRONYMS

ACRONYM	MEANING
BTW	By The Way
FYI	For Your Information
IMHO	In My Honest (or Humble) Opinion
LOL	Laugh Out Loud
RTFL	Read the F_____g (or Fine) Manual
TTYL	Talk To You Later

Also popular among Usenet users are *smileys*, overly cute little symbols to denote feelings of happiness and humor that Usenet users somehow feel unable to express in their articles. (How did Mark Twain and Charles Dickens ever express humor without the use of smileys?) For instance, the following:

:-)

is supposed to represent a smiling face (on its side). Just as often, however, someone will use a smiley when posting an incredible vicious article (called a *flame* in Usenet parlance) and then will try to mediate the damage by throwing a smiley at the end.

Most Usenet rookies are overwhelmed by the Usenet at first, like children in a candy shop, over the amazing assortment of discussion topics. Hours and hours are time spent reading through Usenet newsgroups, until the rookie breaks out of the zombie-like state and realizes, gee, I'm spending a ton of time on the 'Net—and for what?

This guaranteed process means essentially that every rookie will subscribe to every possible group of the barest interest, and then will gradually winnow down to an assortment of truly useful newsgroups. And it's also guaranteed that these useful groups will be in computer-related fields; for instance, as you work to further your knowledge of the UNIX operating system, the UNIX-related newsgroups will make more sense the farther your progress.

Reading Your News

There are many UNIX tools for reading Usenet news: **rn**, **tin**, **trn**, **nn**, **readnews**, **vnews**, **xrn** (a version of **rn** for the X Window System), **xvnews** (a version of **vnews** for the X Window System), and **gnews** and **gnus** (both from the Free Software Foundation). Your system administrator will know which of these newsreaders your system uses.

For the purposes of this discussion, the newsreaders **rn** and **nn** will be covered. Most newsreaders do the same things, such as reading the news and subscribing to newsgroups; it's only the mechanics that differ. Since **rn** is widely available and used by many UNIX users, it will be covered here. Since **nn** is a very good newsreader and can do some things that **rn** can't, it too will be covered here. Even if you have other newsreaders available, the **rn** and **nn** commands are very good for learning the basics of Usenet mail reading. If you're not going to use **rn** or **nn**, however, you should still get something out of this discussion.

Using Rn

Like most UNIX commands, **rn** begins on the command line, usually with no options:

```
$ rn
```

Starting **rn** like this leads to one annoying trait on **rn**'s part: It will ask you if you want to subscribe to any new newsgroups. Since most of us don't want to subscribe to new newsgroups every time we want to read the news, this is indeed annoying behavior. Instead, you may want to start **rn** as in the following:

```
rn -q
```

which goes directly to unread articles.

After you start **rn**, it checks the Usenet files on your system and reports back on the number of unread articles:

```
Unread articles in alt.beer                  24 articles
Unread articles in comp.os.linux            134 articles
Unread articles in comp.unix.questions      211 articles
******24 unread articles in alt.beer --- read now? [ynq]
```

If you hit the **Return** key, you'll be given the first unread article in the first newsgroup on your list—in this case, the first unread article in the **alt.beer** newsgroup. Additional input to **rn** at this point seems pretty simple:

- ▲ Type **y** to read the articles in **alt.beer**.
- ▲ Type **n** to skip the articles in **alt.beer** and move to the news newsgroup, **comp.os.linux**.
- ▲ Type **q** to quit **rn**.

In addition, there are other options not readily apparent from the [*ynq*] command prompt:

- ▲ If you want to see a listing of the subject lines of all unread articles, type = instead of **y**, **n**, or **q** (as shown in Figure 6.3).
- ▲ If you want to look for a specific newsgroup, use a slash (/) or a question mark (?) before the string (such as */unix* to go directly to the first UNIX-related newsgroup).
- ▲ If you want to unsubscribe to a newsgroup, type **u**.
- ▲ To skip all unread articles, type **c** at the [*ynq*] command prompt.

▼

▲ **L E A R N   M O R E   A B O U T** ▲

You can also unsubscribe to newsgroups by editing the
.newsrc file in your home directory. See the section,
"Adding and Eliminating Newsgroups," later in this chapter.

To confuse things a tad, **rn** works in three different modes:

▲ *Newsgroup-selection level*, where you choose which newsgroup to peruse.

▲ *Article-selection level*, where you choose which article to
read (as shown in Figure 6.3) in a particular newsgroup.

▲ *Pager level*, where you're reading a specific article and decid-
ing what to do next.

Why is this confusing? Because each level has its own set of commands.

Some of the commands, such as **n** (which places you in
the next newsgroup), do work in all three levels. Other
commands, such as **p** (which displays the previous newsgroup), work differently depending on the level you're at.

```
Unread articles in alt.beer                24 articles
Unread articles in comp.os.linux          134 articles
Unread articles in comp.unix.questions    211 articles
******24 unread articles in alt.beer—read now? [ynq] =

20456 Summit Pale Ale
20478 Corn or corn products in beers?
20479 Re: Summit Pale Ale
20480 Worst American beer?

What next? [npq]
```

FIGURE 6.3 Listing the articles in article-selection level

▼

To make sense of this confusion, you'll be shown how to perform some basic functions. An overview of all the possible commands is listed in Table 6.3.

TABLE 6.3 COMMAND REFERENCE FOR THE RN COMMAND

rn *option newsgroup*

PURPOSE

The **rn** command allows you to read and send articles to Usenet newsgroups.

OPTION

-q	Starts **rn** without prompting whether to add new newsgroups.

COMMANDS AT THE NEWSGROUP-SELECTION LEVEL

1	Go to the first newsgroup.
$	Go to the last newsgroup.
gnewsgroup	Go to the specified *newsgroup*.
n	Go to the next newsgroup with unread news.
N	Go to the next newsgroup.
p	Go to the previous newsgroup with unread news.
P	Go to the previous newsgroup.
u	Unsubscribe to the current newsgroup.

COMMANDS AT THE ARTICLE-SELECTION LEVEL

n	Go to the next unread article.
N	Go to the next article.
p	Go to the previous unread article.
P	Go to the previous article.
q	Quits the current newsgroup, *not* **rn**.
s *file*	Saves the current message to *file*.
w *file*	Saves the current message to *file*, sans header information.

▼

TABLE 6.3 CONTINUED

num	Go to article *num*.

COMMANDS AT THE PAGER LEVEL

b	Moves back one page.
d	Display the next half page of the message.
j	Move to the next article, marking the current article as read.
q	Goes to the end of the current article.

Once an article is displayed, you have several other options. If you hit the space key, you'll be given the next unread article in the newsgroup on your list; if there are no further unread articles, you'll be moved to the next newsgroup. Other options include:

▲ If you want to look for a specific string in a summary line, use a slash (/) or a question mark (?) before the string (such as */Anchor* to look for information on Anchor Steam in the **alt.beer** newsgroup); the slash tells **rn** to look for articles after the current article, while the question mark tells **rn** to look for articles prior to the current article.

▲ To skip an article after you've started reading it, type **k**.

▲ To skip a current article, all other current articles, and all future articles with the same subject as the original article, use **K**.

You can also respond to a specific post using the **f** and **F** commands. If you choose **f**, the original post is not included in the body of your reply. (This method also allows you to change the topic of your article, so you can scurry off onto a digression if you want. Digressions within the same article subject are highly frowned upon in the Usenet world.) If you choose **F**, the body of the original text *is* included in the body of your reply. (See Figure 6.2 for example of quoted text in a reply.)

There's more to the **rn** command than presented in this section.

▼

To get a full summary of this command, use the **man** command to view **rn**'s online-manual page:

```
$ man rn
```

Using Nn

In many ways, **nn** works similarly to **rn**.

The **nn** command offers a greater level of support when reading through threads. It also allows you more options when configuring and using it, but does add the seemingly requisite level of complexity.

The **nn** command is summarized in Table 6.4.

TABLE 6.4 COMMAND REFERENCE FOR THE NN CCOMMAND

nn *options newsgroup*

PURPOSE

The **nn** command allows you to read and send articles to Usenet newsgroups.

OPTIONS

-i	Makes the **n** and **s** command-line options case-sensitive.
-m	Displays all new articles in all subscribed news-groups in one mondo list.

TABLE 6.4 CONTINUED

-n*string*	Searches for *string* in the author field of articles. (For instance, you could use this command-line option to look for all articles from *reichard*.)
-s*string*	Searches for *string* in the subject field of articles. (For instance, you could use this command-line option to look for all articles about *Summit*.)
-x	Displays all articles in your subscribed newsgroups, even articles you've already read.
-X	Works with other command-line options (such as **m**, which is used in an example elsewhere in this section) to extend the other option to all newsgroups.

COMMANDS WHILE IN SELECTION MODE

space bar	Moves you to the next page of the message. If you've already read the entire message, you'll be moved to the next unread article.
K	Kills the current article in a variety of ways—either killing only the current article or any articles sharing the same subject.
N	Moves to the next group of articles.
P	Moves to the previous group of articles.
Q	Quits **nn**.
U	Unsubscribes the current newsgroup if you subscribe to it; subscribes to the current newsgroup if you don't currently subscribe to it.

COMMANDS IN READING MODE

space bar	Moves down one page in the message, or to the next unread message.
=	Changes your mode from reading to selection.
f	Starts a response to the current post in the form of a newsgroup article.

CHAPTER SIX • The Usenet ▲

k	Kills the remainder of the current thread.
K	Kills the current article in a variety of ways—either killing only the current article or any articles sharing the same subject.
n	Moves you to the next article.
p	Moves you to the previous article.
r	Responds to the creator of the article via e-mail.
s	Saves the item to file.
Q	Quits **nn**.
U	Unsubscribes the current newsgroup if you subscribe to it; subscribes to the current newsgroup if you don't currently subscribe to it.

There are two ways to start **nn**: either going directly to the first newsgroup in your subscription list:

```
$ nn
```

or directly to a specific newsgroup:

```
$ nn alt.beer
```

The **nn** command provides several different ways to view the current articles. The default method—known as *selection mode*—is to list articles along with their subjects and authors; responses to articles and responses to responses are indicated by the > and >> symbols, somewhat like the listing shown in Figure 6.4. In this respect, **nn** is already much handier than **rn**, since **nn** automatically creates groups of messages that share the same subject.

```
$ nn
News group: alt.beer          Articles: 7 of 7/1
a Nine Prosit          ?  Corn or corn products in any beers?
b G. Heileman          5  >
c Kevin Reichard      12  >>
d Eric F. Johnson      ?  Summit Pale Ale
```

```
e David Burnette    55   Erlanger vs. Erdinger
--- 21:07 --- SELECT --- help? --- ALL ---
```

FIGURE 6.4 A typical beginning to an nn session

At this point, you're now in selection mode, and you have quite a few commands available. In this case, *Nine Prosit* created an article called "Corn or corn products in any beers?," and there were two responses—as indicated by the > and >> symbols. The **nn** command organizes articles by letter *(a, b, et al)*, and lists the originator of the article as well as the size of the article (by the number of lines).

The bottom lines gives a status of the **nn** command. Here, you're given the current time, that you're free to select an article to read, that the help system is accessed via the question mark (?), and that you're reading *ALL* new articles in the newsgroup. If not all the articles were displayed on the screen, you would be shown a percentage of the articles displayed so far.

At this point, you can either select a specific article (by pressing the letter at the beginning of the listing—**d** would display Eric F. Johnson's thoughts on Summit Pale Ale beer, for instance) or move to the first unread article. If you hit the space bar, you'll be shown the first article in the queue; hitting the space bar after that will display the articles as listed in Figure 6.4. (You are then placed in reading mode. Ah, the joys of moving through modes.) When you hit the space bar and there are no more articles to read, **nn** quits and you're presented with your command prompt. (Other commands are shown in Table 6.4, the **nn** Command Reference.)

It's possible to tell **nn** to read through every single newsgroup in search of a particular subject. If you're brave, you can use the following command line to start **nn**:

```
$ nn -mX -sunix
```

Here, there are two options to the **nn** command:

▲ The *-mX* option tells **nn** to merge every newsgroup article into a single listing—including newsgroups you don't subscribe to.

▲ The *-sunix* option tells **nn** to search for all articles about *unix*.

You will *never* want to do this, of course—you'd be overwhelmed by the voluminous amount of articles. This is presented merely as an academic exercise.

Getting back to selection mode: You can respond to a specific post using the **f**, **F**, and **r** commands. If you choose **f**, the original post is not included in the body of your reply. (This method also allows you to change the topic of your article, so you can scurry off onto a digression if you want. Digressions within the same article subject are highly frowned upon in the Usenet world.) If you choose **F**, the body of the original text *is* included in the body of your reply. (See Figure 6.2 for example of quoted text in a reply.)

Finally, you can respond to the originator of an article via electronic mail, instead of through a general comment on the Usenet. To do so, type **r** while reading an article. You'll be asked if you want to include the current article (a la the quoted text shown in Figure 6.2); after responding with **y** or **n**, you'll be placed in a text editor (the default is **vi**), where you can compose your response. You'll use the **vi** commands to edit the response (assuming you're using **vi** to compose the response, of course), and you'll use one of the tools supplied to **vi** to quit and save the mail message. After that, however, **nn** will give you another prompt like this:

```
a)bort e)dit h)old m)ail r)eedit s)end v)iew w)rite
Action:
```

Here's your chance to abort the mail (especially if your response is impulsive and nasty), to make some changes to it, or to send it on its merry way.

Adding and Eliminating Newsgroups

There's an easy way to add and delete Usenet newsgroups you've subscribed to—by editing the **.newsrc** file in your home directory, which both **rn** and **nn** uses to track such newsgroups. This is a text file,

▼

so you use the **vi** text editor (or another text editor, if you so choose) to edit this file.

Any file beginning with a period is considered a *hidden* file in UNIX; therefore, they won't appear when you use the **ls** command. To list all files, including hidden files, use the following command:

```
$ ls -a
```

▲ **L E A R N   M O R E   A B O U T** ▲

If you're not familiar with text editing in UNIX, check out the first book in the UNIX Fundamentals series, *UNIX Basics*, for a discussion of UNIX text editing with the **vi** and **emacs** text editors.

Let's say you open the **.newsrc** file and find the following list of files:

```
alt.sex.bizarre:
alt.supermodels:
rec.arts.erotica:
rec.arts.wobegon:
sci.nanotech:
sci.aquaria:
comp.sys.mac:
```

You can edit this file to change the order in which you read the newsgroups and whether or not you subscribe to the group. Let's say you want to drop the erotica and scientific newsgroups, adding discussions of beer and architecture. Your resulting **.newsrc** file would look something like the following:

```
alt.architecture:
alt.beer:
rec.arts.wobegon:
comp.sys.mac:
```

▼

The next time you run **nn** or **rn**, you'd be connected to these newsgroups. With a new newsgroup (and especially a popular newsgroup), it may take a while to compile a list of all unread articles—so be patient.

You may want to temporarily eliminate newsgroups without removing them from the **.newsrc** file. In this case, you'll want to change the colon (:) at the end of each newsgroup to an exclamation point. You can mix and match entries in an **.newsrc file**, as in the following:

```
alt.sex.bizarre:
alt.supermodels:
rec.arts.erotica:
rec.arts.wobegon:
sci.nanotech!
sci.aquaria!
comp.sys.mac:
```

These procedures apply to both the **nn** and **rn** newsgroups, which use the same **.newsrc** file.

There's more to the **nn** command than presented in this section. To get a full summary of this command, use the **man** command to view **nn**'s online-manual page:

```
$ man nn
```

Posting News with Pnews and Postnews

You can also use the **pnews** and **Postnews** commands to post an article to a specific newsgroup, even if you don't personally subscribe to that newsgroup.

▼

The **pnews** and **Postnews** commands will ask you the name of the newsgroup you want to post to, along with the article of your post. Generally speaking, however, you shouldn't go around posting articles to newsgroups you've not familiar with; other Usenet users (and rightfully so) tend to get irritated by the blind requests of people who don't participate in the newsgroup (you could be seen as wanting something without giving something in return—a definite sin in the Usenet world), especially when you ask that queries be answered via electronic mail, since you don't bother to read the newsgroup.

Alternately, you can use the **post** command within **nn** to post an article to a specific newsgroup, even if you don't subscribe to it. After you use the **post** command, **nn** will ask you the name of the newsgroup to post to, followed by a request for the subject, keywords, and summary.

Some Etiquette for Posting to the Usenet

The Usenet has developed into its own insular world, with some veterans wailing about the infusion of "newbies" (new Usenet users) to their little clique. Don't let these wailings bother you—everyone was a newbie once.

However, there are some steps you should take so you don't step on anyone's toes. The Usenet relies on the contributions of everyone, to succeed; if you don't participate in a polite way, you're going to alienate some of the folks needed to make the Usenet hum and purr.

Here are some things to keep in mind when using the Usenet:

▲ **Do Unto Others As They Would Do Unto You.** It's OK to disagree with someone—after all, humankind is built upon disagreements. But there's no reason a disagreement need escalate into something nasty. If you're going to disagree with someone, put the disagreement into nonadversarial terms and don't attack the credibility of the other user—just take polite exception to what they're saying. Including a comment like:

```
Well, moron, you're really a swine if you prefer
that crap Bud to Summit Pale Ale.
```

will inevitably lead them to counterattack, and the entire reason for your original post will be lost in the shuffle (even if the other user *is* a swine for preferring Bud to Summit). And the fault will be yours—in Usenet parlance, you are guilty of flaming the other user. Instead, couch your disagreement in this sort of language:

```
IMHO, Summit Pale Ale is a much better beer than
Budweiser.
```

In short: follow the Golden Rule. Don't send the kind of response that would draw your ire if you received it.

▲ **Read through the entire thread before responding.** You may think it's cool to post a response to a question— and indeed, it is. But make sure no one else has posted the same response already. Read through the entire thread before fashioning your response. There's nothing more irritating than reading through 10 messages, all saying the same thing.

▲ **Get the FAQ, Jack.** Most newsgroups feature a listing of Frequently Asked Questions, or FAQs. They usually contain the answers to your "dumb" questions. (See "Just the FAQs, Ma'am," later in this chapter.)

▲ **Don't expect immediate answers.** Usenet news doesn't travel as fast as electronic mail. As explained in the previous chapter, some system administrators take advantage of lower long-distance rates and grab the Usenet feed in the middle of the night. Your query may not be passed along to the rest of the Usenet until then, and it may take a few days before the entire Usenet has seen your query. Add the few days necessary to get a response back to you, and you may end up waiting a week before anyone responds to your "hot" query.

▲ **Don't expect others to do your work for you.** If you're in college and need advice with a problem, don't expect others to solve your problem for you. (Similarly, don't bug authors of programming books when you've got an important project due and you need someone to solve your mistakes. You'd be amazed how often this happens.) Do your own legwork. If you're still having problems, then ask others for help.

▲ **Be precise in your queries.** The vaguer the question, the less likely you're going to get a usable response. Don't ask someone to explain how to program in C, or to summarize the works of Henry James in 40 words.

▲ **Take it easy with the quoting.** Earlier in this chapter, you learned how to include the text of the article you were responding to. However, don't automatically include the entire text. Take the time to edit down the original article to the section or sections you're responding to, while eliminating other portions.

▲ **Make sure your signature says something.** Many UNIX newsreaders allow you to set up a signature file (the exact file depends on the newsreader, but **.signature** is a common filename), which is merely an ASCII file that contains information about you, as in the following:

```
================================================
Kevin Reichard      reichard@mr.net
1677 Laurel Av.     kreichard@mcimail.com
St. Paul, MN 55104  CServe: 73670,3422
================================================
```

Some people go to great and elaborate lengths with their signature file, including their company, its full address, their many e-mail addresses, and a huge quote apropos of nothing. In many of these cases, these self-centered users have signatures that are larger than the text of their message! Again, keep it short and sweet when it comes to signature files.

Just the FAQs, Ma'am

As Usenet users tired of answering the same questions time and time again, they responded by appointing someone in charge of the Frequently

Asked Questions (FAQs) that are posted periodically to Usenet news-groups. A sample FAQ from the **comp.unix.questions** newsgroup is shown in Figure 6.5.

```
/title News: comp.unix.questions
From tmatimar@isgtec.com 21 Aug 1994 14:46:18 GMT
Path:mr.net!umn.edu!zip.eecs.umich.edu!yeshua.marcam.com!
MathWorks.Com!news2.near.net!bloom-beacon.mit.edu!senator-
bedfellow.mit.edu!faqserv
From: tmatimar@isgtec.com (Ted Timar)
Newsgroups:comp.unix.questions,comp.unix.shell,comp.answers,
news.answers
Subject: Unix - Frequently Asked Questions (1/7) [Frequent
posting]
Supersedes: <unix-faq/faq/part1_776796495@rtfm.mit.edu>
Followup-To: comp.unix.questions
Date: 21 Aug 1994 14:46:18 GMT
Organization: ISG Technologies, Inc
Lines: 390
Approved: news-answers-request@MIT.Edu
Distribution: world
Expires: 18 Sep 1994 14:45:41 GMT
Message-ID: <unix-faq/faq/part1_777480341@rtfm.mit.edu>
References: <unix-faq/faq/contents_777480341@rtfm.mit.edu>
NNTP-Posting-Host: bloom-picayune.mit.edu
X-Last-Updated: 1994/04/28
Originator: faqserv@bloom-picayune.MIT.EDU
Xref: mr.net comp.unix.questions:17140 comp.unix.shell:7319
comp.answers:5151 news.answers:15431

Archive-name: unix-faq/faq/part1
Version: $Id: part1,v 2.5 1994/04/28 19:25:03 tmatimar Exp $

These seven articles contain the answers to some Frequently
Asked Questions often seen in comp.unix.questions and
comp.unix.shell. Please don't ask these questions again,
they've been answered plenty of times already - and please
don't flame someone just because they may not have read this
particular posting. Thank you.
```

Many FAQs, including this one, are available on the archive site rtfm.mit.edu in the directory pub/usenet/news.answers. The name under which a FAQ is archived appears in the "Archive-Name:" line at the top of the article. This FAQ is archived as "unix-faq/faq/part[1-7]".

These articles are divided approximately as follows:

1.*) General questions.
2.*) Relatively basic questions, likely to be asked by beginners.
3.*) Intermediate questions.
4.*) Advanced questions, likely to be asked by people who thought they already knew all of the answers.
5.*) Questions pertaining to the various shells, and the differences.
6.*) An overview of Unix variants.
7.*) An comparison of configuration management systems (RCS, SCCS).

This article includes answers to:

1.1) Who helped you put this list together?
1.2) When someone refers to 'rn(1)' or 'ctime(3)', what does the number in parentheses mean?
1.3) What does {some strange unix command name} stand for?
1.4) How does the gateway between "comp.unix.questions" and the "info-unix" mailing list work?

1.5) What are some useful Unix or C books?

1.6) What happened to the pronunciation list that used to be part of this document?

If you're looking for the answer to, say, question 1.5, and want to skip everything else, you can search ahead for the regular expression "^1.5)".

While these are all legitimate questions, they seem to crop up in comp.unix.questions or comp.unix.shell on an annual basis, usually followed by plenty of replies (only some of which are correct) and then a period of griping about how the same questions keep coming up. You may also like to read the monthly article "Answers to Frequently Asked Questions" in the newsgroup "news.announce.newusers", which will tell you what "UNIX" stands for.

With the variety of Unix systems in the world, it's hard to guarantee that these answers will work everywhere. Read your local manual pages before trying anything suggested here. If you have suggestions or corrections for any of these answers, please send them to tmatimar@isgtec.com.

FIGURE 6.5 The beginning of the comp.unix.questions FAQ

The FAQ quoted in Figure 6.5 is Part 1 of seven separate articles comprising the **comp.unix.questions** FAQ. There's a general summary of the contents of the total package, while elsewhere in the FAQ there will be a more specific index. (In addition, all FAQs are posted to the **news.anwers** newsgroup.)

Also, as noted in Figure 6.5, this FAQ is frequently posted to the **comp.unix.questions** newsgroup; the frequency of FAQs will depend on the newsgroup and who is maintaining the FAQ.

If, after all of this, you still have an unanswered question regarding UNIX, feel free to post it to **comp.unix.questions**. But chances are that your questions can be answered either through this book or through the **comp.unix.questions** FAQ.

▼

Reality Check:
Drawbacks to the Usenet

A dmittedly, the Usenet can be a less-than-ideal source of information. Not every opinion is equal, and there are experts in this world. On the Usenet, the problem is distinguishing between the opinions of the experts and the opinions of the yahoos.

This is not a problem unique to the Usenet, by the way. The issue of the place of the intellectual in modern society is much larger than the Usenet.

On some issues—especially where politics is involved—the Usenet bears an unfortunately resemblance to talk radio. (Indeed, postings from the Usenet are increasingly placed side-by-side in newspapers with opinions from talk radio as some sort of instant examination of the pulse of America.) Discussions are dominated by those who can summon the bluster to drown out those who disagree with them; both are dominated by the conservative portion of the populace, who by nature and definition are those who react the most strongly to any proposed changes in society.

And, quite honestly, neither one means a darn thing in the long run: Talk radio reflects only the opinions of people who aren't making a living at 1 p.m., while the Usenet postings reflects only the opinions of the college students and high-technology workers (the two groups making up the majority of Usenet posters) who have the time to contribute to often meaningless conversations.

Instead, it's best to approach the Usenet on a more practical level: as a source for accurate advice—but not your only source of advice. The UNIX experts who peruse the **comp.unix.questions** newsgroups are always willing to answer your questions. And, depending on your hobby, you'll find that some of the *alt* and *rec* groups can also be valuable sources of information and enjoyment. (Indeed, the authors

▼

have found it highly gratifying to converse with the many thousands of beer lovers in the **alt.beer** newsgroup.) Treat the Usenet as a friendly exchange, in the same manner you'd treat a local users' group, a gathering of friends at a bar, or an assemblage of acquaintances at a coffee shop.

This Chapter in Review

▲ The Usenet is one of the largest free exchanges of information in the world, comprising millions of users and thousands of newsgroups. As such, it's one important component in what's called the Internet.

▲ If you're tied to the Usenet news feed, you can read and send articles to other Usenet users around the world.

▲ Usenet newsgroups are organized by categories (such as *alt* for alternative newsgroups and *comp* for computer-related newsgroups), and from there broken down into smaller, more specific newsgroups (such as **alt.supermodels** and **comp.unix.questions**).

▲ There are many UNIX tools for reading Usenet news. Two of the most common tools are **rn** and **nn**, which are both covered in this chapter.

▲ There are generally accepted rules of conduct when using the Usenet. While most of them are common-sensical— most are variations on the Golden Rule—it wouldn't hurt you to take a minute and review them before diving into the Usenet.

▲ Frequently Asked Questions (FAQs), which are distributed regularly to most newsgroups, are collections of common questions that most users tire of answering. If you're a newcomer and have a question, first check with the FAQ—then post your question to the rest of the world only if you can't find the answer in the FAQ.

▲ There's a definite drawback to relying on the Usenet as your only source of information. Instead, treat it as merely one of many sources of information in your life.

▪ CHAPTER SEVEN ▪

Using Uux, Cu, and Other Communications Commands

There are many additional communications commands associated with the UNIX operating system, including some lesser and additional UUCP commands. Topics in this chapter include:

▲ Running commands remotely with **uux**.

▲ Restrictions placed on the **uux** command.

▲ Practical uses of the **uux** command.

▲ Connecting to other UNIX systems with the **cu** command.

▲ Connecting to non-UNIX systems with the **cu** command.

▲ Online commands for the **cu** command.

▲ Sending files and directories with the **uuto** command.

▲ Receiving files with the **uupick** command.

▲ Using **uustat** to monitor UUCP requests.

▼

More Ways to Connect

In addition to the core UUCP and Usenet commands, the UNIX operating system features a multitude of additional commands for communicating with other computer systems. Some are part of the UUCP suite of commands, while others are merely part of the UNIX operating system. UNIX has an advantage in this sense: While other operating systems must use third-party tools for telecommunications, most of the tools needed for telecommunications are built into UNIX.

This chapter covers two additional, yet important, tools for communicating with other computer systems: **uux** and **cu**. The **uux** command allows you to run commands from a remote machine, while the **cu** command allows you to directly link to a remote machine.

Running Commands Remotely with Uux

The **uux** command allows you to run a command on a remote system and then display the output from that command on your system. The remote system must be part of your UUCP network, which means it must be listed in the **Systems** file and returned by the **uuname** file (both of which you learned about in Chapter 5). The **uux** command is summarized in Table 7.1.

TABLE 7.1 COMMAND REFERENCE FOR THE UUX COMMAND

uux *options system!command*

PURPOSE

The **uux** command allows you run commands on a remote machine. (The commands are usually limited by the remote machine; a listing of permissible commands can be often be found on a remote system in **etc/uucp/permissions**.) In addition, it allows you to send and receive files from remote systems.

▼

OPTIONS

-a*user*	Notify *user* when command is completed.
-b	Returns the input if an error interrupts the *command*.
-c	Copy the actual file, not a copy from the spool file.
-C	Copy to a spooling file before sending on to the destination machine.
-g*p*	Set job priority to *p*.
-j	Print **uux** job number.
-n	Do not send mail if the *command* fails.
-p	Use standard input for *command*.
-r	Queue the *file(s)*, but don't send them.
-s*file*	Send the transfer status to *file* (instead of to user, as specified by **-m**.) (Not available on all systems.)
-z	Notify user who initiated command when it is completed.

In theory, the **uux** command should allow you a great amount of power. In reality, you don't have a lot of power, as the commands you can run from the remote machine are usually quite limited. Why? *Security*. A system administrator should cringe at the thought of a beginning user like yourself having access to commands like **rm ***, which would remove every file on the remote machine. That's why the **uux** command has evolved into a tool for working with files, as well as for sharing resources among the users of a larger network.

The actual permissions on a remote machine are stored in **/etc/uucp/permissions,** which is not usually readable by all users. A command must be enabled by both the remote and local machines before it can be used via the **uux** command—so in essence you may be fumbling around in the dark a lot before you actually run into a command you can use. To see which commands can be executed with **uux** on your end, you'll need to check with your system administrator.

Because of these restrictions, you're essentially limited to some very basic UNIX commands. Still, there are some useful purposes for **uux**. For instance, you can gather a file from a remote machine and combine it with a file on your local system using the **cat** command (which is usually available via **uux**). The following command grabs the file **carter** from the remote machine *vikings* and the file **lions** from the remote machine *lions* and combines them into the file **favre** on the machine *packers*.

```
$ uux "!cat vikings!/home/cris/carter
lions!/home/johnny/cash > packers!/home/bret/favre"
```

The machine names in this chapter are pure gibberish. Don't bother trying to use them on your machine.

The quirks of the **uux** can be somewhat confusing. For instance, if you want to run a local command, you must begin it with an exclamation point. In the previous example, the **!cat** means that you're running the **cat** command locally, not on a remote system. The quotation marks are necessary if you use any of the UNIX redirection commands—>, <, ;, and |—since they are special shell commands.

Connecting Directly to Other Systems with Cu

If your UNIX system is set up correctly—as always, a matter for your system administrator to determine—you can directly call another computer system, whether or not it's running UNIX. This remote system must be able to display everything in text, rather than graphics (so you could call a text-based system like CompuServe or Delphi, but not a graphical-based system like America Online or eWorld).

The **cu** makes such communications possible. **Cu** is quite simple to use, really—all you do is specify the number of the remote machine and login. Of course, you must make sure that you have an account on the remote machine, which usually involves a username and a password.

Users of Berkeley-based UNIX have a functional equivalent, called **tip**, on their systems. However, the vast majority of UNIX users have access to the **cu** command, so this chapter will cover **cu** and not **tip**.

The **cu** command can be used to connect both to UUCP machines and to non-UNIX computers. Since in most cases you'll want to connect to non-UNIX machines, this chapter will begin with a discussion of these connections, followed by a discussion of using **cu** with UUCP machines.

The **cu** command is summarized in Table 7.2.

TABLE 7.2 COMMAND REFERENCE FOR THE CU COMMAND

cu *options system*

PURPOSE

The **cu** command tells your UNIX system to connect directly to another UNIX system or terminal, or non-UNIX bulletin-board service or online service, via modem or direct line.

OPTIONS

-b*n*	Sets bit length to 7 or 8.
-c*name*	Searches the **Device** file for *name*.

▼

TABLE 7.2 CONTINUED

-d	Sets diagnostics mode.
-e	Sets even parity. (Opposite of -o.)
-h	Sets half-duplex.
-l*port*	Specifies specific port for communications.
-n	Prompts the user for a telephone number.
-o	Sets odd parity. (Opposite of -e.)
-s*rate*	Sets bits-per-second rate (300, 1200, 2400, 9600, et al).
-t	Calls an ASCII terminal.

Dialing Direct

In many cases you'll use the **cu** command to connect directly to an online service (such as CompuServe or MCI Mail) or a local bulletin-board system (BBS). In these cases, you'll need to specify the phone number of the remote system, as well as some technical parameters.

For instance, you may want to use your UNIX system to call MCI Mail, a popular electronic-mail service. MCI Mail is text-based and uses 800 numbers for dialing in. Additionally, MCI offers access up to 9600 bits per second (bps), so you can do a high-speed check of your electronic mail.

This is technical

Communication speeds are measured in bits per second, or bps. This is a more accurate measurement than baud, which many computer users are familiar with. However, baud and bps aren't the same unless you're talking about slower speeds, such as 1200 baud.

Before you can call MCI Mail, there are a few pieces of information you'll need:

- ▲ The telephone number for establishing the link with MCI Mail.
- ▲ Your username and password on the remote system.
- ▲ Whether or not you're dialing out of a PBX.
- ▲ The speed you'll be using to establish the connection.

The first two items are supplied by MCI Mail. The third item is supplied by your system administrator. The fourth item is a combination of both—many online services have a ceiling on bps speeds (MCI Mail, for instance, allows connections only up to 9600 bps), while your modem may be slower than these maximum connection rates. You'll need to choose the lower rate of the two. (If you don't specify a bps rate, **cu** will go ahead and use the default rate for that port.)

If you're calling out over a modem, you'll also have to insert a Hayes command, telling the modem to open a phone line and a dial tone.

This is technical

Hayes commands are direct instructions to a modem. Check with your system administrator to see if you need to use any Hayes commands with your particular modem.

Putting all of this together, we can call MCI Mail at 9600 bps through the system's modem using the following command line:

```
$ cu -s9600 ATDT18009679600
```

The *-s9600* indicates the bps rate. (There are additional options for the **cu** command, as listed in Table 7.2.) The *ATDT* tells the modem to open the phone line and establish a dial tone. The *18009679600* is the telephone number for MCI Mail.

▼

You can put hyphens between elements of the phone number, in the same manner in which a phone number is listed in the real world. The hyphen is in theory a pause in the dialing of a phone number, according to **cu** documentation (although the exact length of the pause depends on the version of the documentation—between 1 and 4 seconds, by some accounts). If you use hyphens in your phone number, you must place the entire phone number within quotation marks:

```
$ cu "1-800-967-9600"
```

If you don't use the quotation marks, the shell will assume that the hyphens are shell commands—and this will definitely lead to some unintended results.

There are also situations where you'll need to dial *9 to get an outside line. Since you don't want the asterisk to be interpreted in some unwanted way by the shell, you will have to surround the number within quotation marks:

```
$ cu "*9=1-800-967-9600"
```

If you had been dialing out of a company PBX, you would have used the following command line:

```
$ cu -s9600 ATDT9=18009679600
```

The addition of *9=* tells the modem to dial *9* (which is what PBXes use to access an outside line) and to wait for a dial tone before dialing the rest of the number.

The exact string you'll use—such as whether you'll need an *ATDT* within your command line—depends on your system configuration. As always, check with your system administrator about the specific commands needed to call out with your particular system.

If your connection was successful, your screen will look like this:

```
$ cu -s9600 ATDT9=1-800-967-9600
connected

CONNECT 9600/V42BIS

Pad ID: N4.1 - Port: 41
Please enter your user name: kreichard
Password:
COM

Welcome To MCI Mail!

Out of stamps?  MCI solves that
problem:  Send an MCI letter to
anyone in the world straight
from your PC.

Type HELP ADDRESS PAPER for
details.

Today's Headlines at 4 pm EDT

—Kodak Sells Health-Products Unit
    To SmithKline For $2.9 Billion
—MCI Calls Off $1.3 Billion Deal
    To Acquire Stake In Nextel

Type //BUSINESS on Dow Jones for details.

MCI Mail Version V13.0.B

    There are 2 messages waiting in your INBOX.

Command:
```

Once you are connected, you may have to hit the **Return** key a few times before the remote system sends you anything; some online services, such as MCI Mail, need those **Return**s to get their communications parameters aligned. That's normal and part of the process.

Every UNIX configuration is different. On your system, you may need to specify a port number to call out from. You may need to add some other characters to call out. Or you may not even be able to call out at all. As always, check with your system administrator about the specific steps needed to use the **cu** command.

Using Cu with UUCP Connections

You may want to directly login one of the computers listed in the **Systems** file (and accessed with the **uuname** command), which you learned about in Chapter 5. To do this, you can just specify the name of the system on the command line:

```
$ cu mtxinu

Connected
login:
password:

mtxinu%
```

The above interaction actually encompasses a few steps. Your original command of **cu mtxinu** is followed by a pause, as your system attempts to connect with the remote system. This connection may take place through a direct connection, over a modem, or through a gateway connecting your local network to a larger network. The specifics of this connection is kept in the **Systems** file, and you don't need to know the specifics.

As you wait for the connection, there's no feedback: You don't know what the modem is doing (if indeed the connection is being made via modem), you don't know if the line is busy, you don't know if the remote system is busy, and so on.

When a connection is made, you're told so by the *Connected*. At this point, you'll be asked for a username, and a password. This username and password is actually the username for your system, not yourself personally (see your system administrator for these details). Finally, you'll be presented with a prompt on the remote machine. At this point, you can enter any UNIX commands.

A similar setup can be used for non-UNIX machines. There's nothing to prevent you from specifying a non-UNIX machine in the **Systems** file on your system. While you probably don't have permission to change that file—a good system administrator saves that privilege so the important file isn't wrecked—you can ask your system administrator to add frequently used online services to that file. For instance, if you plan on regularly accessing MCI Mail from your UNIX terminal, you can ask your system administrator to add *MCI* to the **Systems** file. The next time you connect with MCI Mail, you can use *MCI* as the name of the remote machine, instead of typing out the entire phone number of MCI Mail:

```
$ cu mci

Connected
CONNECT 9600/V42BIS

Pad ID: N4.1 - Port: 41
Please enter your user name: kreichard
Password:
COM

Welcome To MCI Mail!

Out of stamps?  MCI solves that
problem:  Send an MCI letter to
anyone in the world straight
from your PC.

Type HELP ADDRESS PAPER for
details.

Today's Headlines at 4 pm EDT

—Kodak Sells Health-Products Unit
      To SmithKline For $2.9 Billion
```

▼

```
—MCI Calls Off $1.3 Billion Deal
     To Acquire Stake In Nextel

 Type //BUSINESS on Dow Jones for details.

MCI Mail Version V13.0.B

     There are no messages waiting in your INBOX.

Command:
```

If *MCI* isn't listed in the **Systems** file, you'll get an error message like this:

```
Connect failed: Requested device/system name not known.
```

Cu Commands

Once you're connected to a remote system, you can interact directly with it and issue commands. Once connected to MCI Mail, for instance, you can scan for new messages or post mail to another electronic-mail user. MCI Mail doesn't care if the commands come from a PC, a Macintosh, or a UNIX box, so long as they are valid MCI Mail commands. The same goes for other text-based online services and BBSes.

Cu also features a number of commands that affect local usage. These commands begin with a tilde (~) character and are quite useful. They are listed in Table 7.3.

TABLE 7.3 ONLINE COMMANDS FOR THE CU COMMAND

COMMAND	PURPOSE
~!*command*	Runs *command* on the local system.
~$*command*	Runs *command* on the local system and then send the output to the remote system.
~%cd *directory*	Changes to directory *directory* on local system.
~%put *file*	Copies *file* from the local system to the remote system.

~$take *file*	Takes *file* from the remote system and places it on the local system.
~!	Exits **cu**.
~.	Disconnects the telephone link between the two systems.
~?	Displays a listing of all online commands.

For instance, you may connect to a remote computer and encounter some problems where you can't end the connection. However, you do have a command on your end that severs the connection with the remote machine and returns you back to the UNIX prompt:

```
remote% ~.
```

followed by the **Return** key.

Additional Command when Working With a UNIX System

Since **cu** is used primarily to exchange files with other UNIX systems, it's no surprise that the majority of **cu** online commands are devoted to the exchange of files.

Most of these commands operate along some consistent lines: You *put* files on a remote system, and you *take* files from a remote system. Therefore, it's no surprise that the command to copy a file to a remote system is:

```
remote% ~%put file
```

where *file* is the name of the file to be copied. The command to copy a file from a remote system is:

```
remote% ~%take file
```

where *file* is the name of the file to be copied.

In theory, these tilde commands can be used with non-UNIX systems, so long as the non-UNIX systems support the **echo**, **stty**, and **cat** commands.

Reality Check: What Can Go Wrong With Cu

Though it's a handy command at times, the **cu** command is far from perfect. For starters, it relies totally on hardware when connecting to a remote location. This means a reliance on a modem to sustain a connection. And it means a reliance on clean telephone lines to further sustain that connection.

Of course, you need initial access to a modem before even trying that connection. If there are only a few modems connected to your system and many people interested in dialing up an online service, you may find yourself in some competition for those modems. The trouble is, **cu** offers no feedback as to what modems and ports are available. All you can do is try a port and see what happens. If the port is busy, you'll get an error message like the following:

```
Connect failed: No device available
```

And even when you think you've made a connection, the lack of feedback may lead to some misinformation from **cu**. If things appear to freeze, it could be that the remote system's telephone line was busy—but **cu** has no way of telling you that. Since the modem is probably in another part of the office, you can't listen to the modem or watch the lights for feedback.

To make things worse, most **cu**-based communications occur without the benefit of some sort of error-checking. By contrast, much of the data transfer that occurs with the Usenet and electronic mail are validated by the use of error-checking. With **cu**, you're at the mercy of good modems and clean telephone lines—so it's no surprise you occasionally end up with a screen of garbage as line noise makes its way to you. And even when a connection is good, screen garbage occurs when there's a mismatched connection between the two systems. If you continue to have problems with garbage-filled screens, check with your system administrator.

Other Communications Commands

The UUCP suite of commands encompasses a few lesser commands that may be useful in some limited situations: **uuto**, **uupick**, and **uustat**.

Transferring Files with Uuto

The **uuto** command allows you to send a file, multiple files, or an entire directory to another machine that's listed in your **Systems** file and returned by the **uuname** command (both of which you learned about in Chapter 5). Actually, the **uuto** command is one of the handiest UNIX communications commands—it's relatively efficient, it's easy to use, and it almost always works. The **uuto** command is summarized in Table 7.4.

TABLE 7.4 COMMAND REFERENCE FOR THE UUTO COMMAND

uuto *options file(s) destination*

PURPOSE
The **uuto** command copies files and directories from your system to another UUCP-connected system.

OPTIONS

-m	Sends you mail when the file transfer is completed.
-p	Copies files to the spool directory.

The basic mechanism for **uuto** is simple: You specify a file, a remote machine to send that file to, and the name of the user who's

▼

the *ostensible* recipient of the file. The term *ostensible* is used here because the file will be copied to a public directory (usually **/var/spool/uucppublic**, but it may differ on your system) on the remote system, and the specified user will be told via electronic mail that a file has been sent. For instance, the following command line will send the file **vikings** to the user *carter* on the machine *moon:*

```
$ uuto vikings moon!carter
```

The user *carter* will be informed by mail when the file is transferred.

You can also specify a bang path if you want to send your file through a series of machines. However, in this instance, you must know that the string of machines are indeed connected via UUCP; UNIX is an unforgiving operating system, and if your request fails along the way, you'll never know when, how, or why. For example, the following command line will send the file **vikings** to the user *carter* through the machines *moon, lee, allen,* and *thomas:*

```
$ uuto vikings moon!lee!allen!thomas!carter
```

If you want to send the contents of an entire directory, you can specify the name of the directory instead of a filename. For example, the following command line will send the entire contents of the direc tory **reports** to the user *carter* on the machine *moon:*

```
$ uuto reports moon!carter
```

There are two convenient options to the **uuto** command, and you may want to consider using both of them every time you use **uuto:**

▲ The *-m* option sends you mail after the file has been transferred.

▲ The *-p* copies the files to a spool directory, where they await transfer.

The rationale for the *-m* option is self-explanatory. However, the rationale behind the *-p* option may not be readily apparent, until you learn a little how **uuto** works. When you ask **uuto** to transfer a file, the actual transfer may not be made immediately. **Uuto** copies the file as it is when the physical transfer is made. If you make a **uuto** request at 9 a.m. and the actual transfer doesn't take place until 11 a.m., **uuto** will copy the file as it exists at 11 a.m. If you've made changes to the file between 9 a.m. and 11 a.m., those changes will be reflected in the file sent via **uuto**.

The -*p* option tells **uuto** to copy the file as it exists when you make the **uuto** request into a separate spool directory. (In computerese, a spool directory is a temporary directory where file exist before they are acted upon. When you print a file and there's a long gap between when you make the print request and when the file is actually printed, the file is temporarily stored in a spool directory.) When the actual **uuto** transfer takes place, the file in the spool directory is copied, not the file as it may exist elsewhere on your UNIX system.

Receiving Files with Uupick

If you're the recipient of the file sent via **uuto**, you'll be notified that the file has arrived via electronic mail.

While you can use the standard UNIX commands to move or copy the file from the UUCP public directory, there's a handier tool to retrieve these files: the **uupick** command, as summarized in Table 7.5.

TABLE 7.5 COMMAND REFERENCE FOR THE UUPICK COMMAND

uupick *option*

PURPOSE
The **uupick** command grabs files sent from a remote system.

OPTION
-s *system*   Checks for files sent from *system.*

▼

TABLE 7.5 CONTINUED

COMMANDS	
*	Prints all available commands.
!command	Runs shell *command*.
a	Retrieves all files meant for you from a specific system.
d	Deletes the file.
m	Moves the file to your current *directory*.
m *dir*	Moves the file to directory.
p	Print the file.
q	Quits the **uupick** command.

Again, **uupick** is not an exceptionally complex command; like most UNIX tools, it was created to perform one very specific task. In this case, all **uupick** does is retrieve files to your current directory after they were sent with **uuto**. (This is a point that trips up many **uupick** beginners—the files are transferred to your current directory, not your home directory.) When you run **uupick**, the command will run through a list of the files sent to you via **uuto** and ask you what you want to do with them:

```
$ uupick
from system oiler: file vikings ?
```

You have a number of commands available at this point (which are summarized in Table 7.5). Generally speaking, though, you'll want to either move the file or delete the file. If you want to move the file, type **m** in response to the **uupick** query:

```
$ uupick
from system oiler: file vikings?
m
10 blocks
```

▼

If you were to specify another directory with the **m** command, the file would be moved to that directory:

```
$ uupick
from system oiler: file vikings?
m /temp
10 blocks
```

If you wanted to move all of the files sent from the current system (in the case of our examples, *oiler*), you'd use the following commands:

```
$ uupick
from system oiler: file vikings?
a
2110 blocks
```

If you have many systems sending you files, you can pick and choose from the different systems with the *-s* option. For instance, to view only the files sent the system *lions*, you'd use the following command line:

```
$ uupick -s lions
from system lions: file defense?
```

Using Uustat to Monitor UUCP Requests

As you learned in the section "Transferring Files with Uuto," not every **uucp** request is immediately honored, due to a variety of factors.

If you want to check on the status of your **uucp** request (known in these circumstances as *jobs*), use the **uustat** command, summarized in Table 7.6.

▼

TABLE 7.6 COMMAND REFERENCE FOR THE UUSTAT COMMAND

> **uustat** *options*
>
> **PURPOSE**
>
> The **uustat** command details the status of **uucp** requests and can be used to cancel them if necessary.
>
> **OPTIONS**
>
> -a   Reports on all **uucp** requests, not just yours.
>
> -k*jobID*   Kills *jobID*, if you're the owner of the request.
>
> -q   Reports on the jobs for all systems.
>
> -s*system*   Reports on the status of jobs meant for *system*.

The **uustat** command is pretty simple—you can use it to monitor and cancel jobs. Running it without any options gives you the status of jobs you've originated:

```
$ uustat
vikiD3ly7 08/31-10:49 S vikings geisha  1024  /home/vikings
```

The information returned by **uustat** goes as follows:

- ▲ *vikiD3ly7* is the job-ID of the **uucp** request; you'll need this ID if you want to kill the job.
- ▲ *08/31-10:49* is the time the request was made.
- ▲ *S* refers to whether the request was to send a file (indicated by *S*) or receive a file (indicated by *R*).
- ▲ *vikings* is the system where the file is to be sent.
- ▲ *geisha* is the user requesting the transfer.
- ▲ *1024* is the size of the file.
- ▲ */home/vikings* is the name of the file being transferred.

To kill this request, you'd combine the **uustat** command with the -*k* option and the job ID:

```
$ uustat -k vikiD3ly7
UX: Job: vikiD3ly7 - successfully killed
```

▼

This Chapter in Review

▲ There are a variety of additional UNIX communications commands that sometimes fall through the cracks. Still, under certain circumstances, these commands can be quite useful.

▲ The **uux** command, in theory, allows you to run commands on remote machines. However, the practicalities dictate otherwise—security concerns prevent the use of most UNIX commands, except harmless commands like **cat**.

▲ The **cu** command allows you to connect to remote systems via direct link, modem, or network connection.

▲ If a system is listed in the **Systems** file, the connection can be made by combining the system name with the **cu** command on a command line.

▲ The **cu** command can also be used to communicate directly with non-UNIX systems, such as online services and bulletin-board systems. In this case, you'll need to tell the modem exactly what to do (such as setting the bits-per-second rate) and the phone number to call. In addition, these non-UNIX systems must display only in text (such as CompuServe or MCI Mail), not graphics (such as Prodigy or America Online).

▲ The **uuto** command allows you to send a file or directory to a remote system, to a public directory.

▲ The **uupick** command allows you to move files sent to you via the **uuto** command.

▲ The **uustat** commands lets you monitor UUCP requests and, if necessary, kill them.

▪ CHAPTER EIGHT ▪

Communicating With Other Network Users

What good is a network if you can't communicate directly with the other users? UNIX features several command that allow you to communicate directly with other users. In addition, UNIX features commands that allow you to send files to and from remote systems. Topics in this chapter include:

▲ Cutting through the jargon of networking.

▲ Using the **who** command to see who else is logged on the system.

▲ Using the **rwho** command to see who else is logged on the system.

▲ Using the **finger** command to find out more about a network user.

▲ Using the **write** command to send an instant message to another user.

▲ Using the **talk** command to chat with another networked user.

▲ Blocking chat requests with the **mesg** command.

▲ The Berkeley Remote commands.

▼

▲ Using **rlogin** to login a remote system.

▲ Using the **rcp** command to copy systems to and from a remote system.

Some Notes About Networking

There are some UNIX users and system administrators who do their darndest to make the UNIX operating system as complicated as possible, especially when it comes to networking considerations. They really expect you to care what networking protocol is being used on your UNIX system (such as TCP/IP), whether your network is really a local-area network (LAN) or wide-area network (WAN), and how well your network adheres to the Open System Interconnection (OSI) Reference model. They also will throw terms like *mount* and *firewalls* at you, as if you really cared—or that it really matters as you do your daily work.

While you don't need to be a technical expert to use the UNIX operating system—despite the reputation that exists in the greater computing community—you should have a little idea about how your network works. More importantly, you should know about the features of the network that you can directly use to interact with other network users. You've already seen some of this with electronic mail; now you'll see it through direct messages to other users on your network.

Notes To Fellow Users

There's a host of commands that allow you to directly communicate with other users on the network. These commands are pretty simple and don't require a ton of expertise on your part.

The Who Command

These commands tend to be limited in scope and designed for a very specific purpose (much like the greater world of UNIX commands).

An example of this is the **who** command. The **who** command returns the names of the users currently logged on your network. It's pretty simple to use:

```
$ who
big_bird    term/02    Aug 12 08:42
geisha      term/12    Aug 12 11:10
reichard    term/08    Aug 12 09:14
bert        term/11    Aug 12 08:55
ernie       term/10    Aug 12 07:15
```

This tells you who else is logged on the system (in this case, a system located on Sesame Street), along with a lot of information you'll never use, such as when the user logged on the system and what terminal they're using.

The **who** command is summarized in Table 8.1.

TABLE 8.1 COMMAND REFERENCE FOR THE WHO COMMAND

who *options file*

PURPOSE

The **who** command displays the names and other information about users logged on the system.

OPTIONS

am I	Displays who you are (your system name).
-a	Uses all options listed here.
-b	Returns the last time and date the system was booted.
-d	Returns expired processes.
-H	Inserts column headings.
-l	Returns lines available for login.
-n*n*	Displays *n* users per line.

▼

TABLE 8.I CONTINUED

-p	Returns processes started by **init** that are still active.
-q	Quick who; displays only usernames.
-r	Returns run level.
-s	Returns name, line, and time fields (default).
-t	Returns the last time the system clock was updated with **clock**.
-T	Returns the state of each terminal:
	+ Any user can write to the terminal
	1- Only system administrator can write to the terminal
	? Error with the terminal.
-u	Returns terminal usage in idle time.

The Rwho Command

Similar to the **who** command is the **rwho** command, which also lists all users currently logged on the system.

The **rwho** command is not available on all systems, however, and some system administrators choose not to make it accessible at all times.

The **rwho** command is summarized in Table 8.2.

▼

TABLE 8.2 COMMAND REFERENCE FOR THE RWHO COMMAND

rwho *option*

PURPOSE

The **rwho** command shows who is logged on all machines on the network.

OPTION

-a   Includes all users, even those whose machines have been idle for more than an hour.

The Finger Command

Once you see who's logged on the network, you can find out more regarding a user than just the username.

For instance, many larger companies require that their users create a little database that sums up their personal corporate information, such as their phone number and their full names.

You can access this information with the **finger** command. Using the information returned by **who**, as previously listed in this chapter, you can use **finger** to learn about a user you don't know much about. Using the command on the user enigmatically named **geisha**, you would run a command line like the following:

```
$ finger geisha
Login name: geisha  In real life: Geisha The Cat
(612) 555-5555
Directory: /home/geisha    Shell: /usr/bin/csh
Last login Thu Sep 1 08:45 on term/12
Project: Feline Computing Tools
```

Don't be surprised if the **finger** command doesn't give you this much information on your network, however. Most system administrators on midsized or smaller systems don't place a high priority on this command—which is understandable, given the fact that in a smaller company, everyone tends to know everyone anyway.

The **finger** command is summarized in Table 8.3.

TABLE 8.3 COMMAND REFERENCE FOR THE FINGER COMMAND

finger *options user(s)*

PURPOSE

The **finger** command returns information about users with accounts on the system: Username, full name, terminal, terminal access, time of login, and phone number. In addition, **finger** grabs information from the user's login shell, **.plan** file, and **.project** file. Information is returned in long display or short display.

The **finger** command will search for information based on a specific username or general first and last names. For instance, a search of the name of *smith* on a large system will probably yield quite a few responses.

The use of the **finger** command with no username will return a list of all users currently logged on the system.

OPTIONS

-b   Long display, without information about home directory and shell.

-f   Short display, sans header.

-h   Long display, without information gleaned from the **.project** file.

-i   Shows "idle" status: username, terminal, time of login, and idle lines.

-l   Long display.

-m   Matches the username exactly, with no searching of first or last names.

-p	Long display, without information gleaned from the **.plan** file.
-q	Quick display of username, terminal, and time of login (with no searching of first or last names).
-s	Short format.
-w	Short format, without the user's first name.

Be sure and specify the name of a user with the **finger** command, particularly if you're working on a larger system. Using **finger** by itself on the command line will return the names of *all* the users on your system.

The Write Command

Once you've found out **geisha**'s real name and project, you may want to drop her a note and introduce yourself.

You can send a single message to another users logged on the system with the **write** command. The message will appear on the other user's screen. There's no interactivity here (you can do that with the **talk** command, which is referenced later in this chapter).

For instance, you may want to ask **geisha** about the status of her research. You would do so with the following command line and subsequent message:

```
$ write geisha
Hello nurse! How's the research going?
Ctrl-D
```

Using **write** is pretty simple: You enter the name of the other user, type your message, and end it with a **Ctrl-D**.

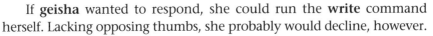

If **geisha** wanted to respond, she could run the **write** command herself. Lacking opposing thumbs, she probably would decline, however.

The **write** command is summarized in Table 8.4.

TABLE 8.4 COMMAND REFERENCE FOR THE WRITE COMMAND

write *user tty*

PURPOSE
Sends a text message to another user. Use **Ctrl-D** to exit.

OPTIONS
None.

The Talk Command

The **write** command sends a single message to another network user. Newer versions of UNIX, however, feature a new command for carrying on an interactive chat session with another user.

If you felt like striking up a conversation with **geisha**, you could use the **talk** command to chat with her. The **talk** command splits the screen into two areas: The top contains the lines you type and send off to **geisha,** while the bottom half contains **geisha**'s responses. To run **talk**, you'd use a command line like the following:

```
$ talk geisha
```

Geisha would see a message like the following on her screen:

```
Message from Talk_Daemon@spike at 8:55
talk: connection requested by kevin@spike
talk: respond with talk kevin@spike
```

If **geisha** did indeed want to carry on a conversation, she'd run the following command line:

```
$ talk kevin@spike
```

The conversation would then commence.

To end the conversation, press the **Del** key or the **Ctrl-D** keys.

Not all systems feature or implement the **talk** command. Some system administrators, in order to preserve precious system resources, disable this command. In the above message to **geisha**, alerting her that **kevin** wanted to talk, it was the *Talk_daemon* informing her of that fact. A *daemon* is a UNIX process, running in the background until specifically called by a user. Many of the other commands in this section, such as **rwho**, rely on a daemon to work. To cut down on the number of *daemons* and save on system resources, many system administrators choose not to run them.

The **talk** command is summarized in Table 8.5.

TABLE 8.5 THE COMMAND REFERENCE FOR THE TALK COMMAND

talk *username[@hostname] terminal*

PURPOSE

The **talk** command allows you to carry on a conversation with another user on the network. The command splits your screen into two areas: The top half contains your typing, and the bottom contains messages from the other user.

The **write** command is similar, except that **write** is geared for single messages and not for an ongoing dialog.

Use **Ctrl-D** or **Del** to exit.

OPTIONS

user	Other user, obviously.
hostname	The *hostname* of the machine the *user* is logged on, if the user isn't logged in to your local machine.
terminal	Specified a *tty* should the *user* be logged on more than one terminal.

The Mesg Command

There may be times when you don't want to chat with other users, partucularly when you're trying to get some real work done.

If you don't want to be bothered by people using the **talk** and **write** commands, you can refuse them entry to your terminal screen with the **mesg** command. To deny **write** and **talk** permission, you'd run the following command line:

```
$ mesg -n
```

Once someone tried to flag you down with **write** or **talk**, they'd get the following response:

```
Permission denied.
```

To give others the chance to chat with you, you'd use the following command line:

```
$ mesg -y
```

The **mesg** command is summarized in Table 8.6.

TABLE 8.6 COMMAND REFERENCE FOR THE MESG COMMAND

mesg *options*

PURPOSE

The **mesg** command grants or denies permission to other users to send you messages via the **write** or **talk** commands.

OPTIONS

-n	Forbids messages.
-y	Allows messages.

The Berkeley Remote Commands

Another important set of networking tools are the Berkeley remote commands.

First introduced in the BSD strains of UNIX, these remote commands (sometimes referred to as **R** commands, as they all begin with the letter r) allow you to communicate with remote systems. They're not as extensive as the **ftp** and **telnet** command covered in the next chapter, but they are still useful for extending the reach of your network.

Here's one case where knowing your network scheme actually is relevant. Throughout this book, and particularly in Chapter 5, you've been working with commands that assume there's a UUCP connection between your computer and other computers. The **R** commands rely on TCP/IP, however. TCP/IP, short for *Transmission Control Protocol/Internet Protocol*, is a widely used networking protocol used to link computers of all sorts. They don't need to be running the UNIX operating system to use TCP/IP/.

> ▲ L E A R N M O R E A B O U T ▲
>
> TCP/IP serves as the central protocol for the vast array of computers known as the Internet, which you'll cover in Chapter 9.

However, the **R** commands do rely on the remote system running the UNIX operating system. They also rely on both the remote system and your system being set up to allow your access to the remote machine. On the remote machine, the file **/etc/host.equiv** must be set up to allow your machine to login. You don't have any power over that system, and permissions must be set by the remote system administrator.

However, the security on your own system may have a few variations. You may have a file called **.rhosts** in your home directory. This file specifies who can log on your machine and directory, and also what remote machines you're allowed to login. However, larger systems typically don't allow individual users to control their own remote permissions; the files may exist in your home directory, but only the system administrator has the power to change these files. As always, you should check with your system administrator before using advanced networking commands.

Using the R commands

Assuming that you have the proper permissions, you have access to some very useful **R** commands.

One of the most useful is the ability to login remote machines. There are several circumstances where this is handy:

▲   You're overseeing a large project where several team members are storing their contributions on remote machines, and it's your task to combine their contributions.

▲   You're sharing financial information with a remote subsidiary.

▲   You, as well as many other users, need access to information generated at another site.

You do so with the **rlogin** command. To login the remote system, you first need permission to do so. This must be set up by the system administrator of the remote system, who will typically assign you a username and password. Also, your privileges on the remote machine will typically be confined to access to specific directories and specific UNIX commands. While there's a lot of activity that goes on to ensure your ability to login the remote machine, you won't need to deal with much of it.

To login the remote machine, you'd specify the name of the machine on the command line:

```
$ rlogin remote
```

where *remote* is the name of the remote machine. While connected, you can move between files (using the *cd* command) and copy files to and from the remote machine.

To end the **rlogin** connection, use **Ctrl-D** or **exit**.

The **rlogin** command is summarized in Table 8.7.

TABLE 8.7 COMMAND REFERENCE FOR THE RLOGIN COMMAND

rlogin *options hostname*

PURPOSE

The **rlogin** command logs you on a remote system. A list of the available *hostnames* is stored in the **/etc/hosts/.rhosts** file. If your *local* hostname is listed in the **.rhosts** file in your home directory on the *remote* machine, then you won't have to enter a password.

Your local computing session is suspended when you're logged on a remote machine. Any UNIX commands you use will be run on the remote machine.

When you're finished on the remote system, use an **exit** command or type **Ctrl-D** to end the connection.

OPTIONS

-8	Use 8-bit data (default is 7 bits).
-e *c*	Use *c* as the default escape character (default is ~).
-l *username*	Remotely login under the new *username*, instead of the name on your local host.

Using Rcp

You don't need to login a remote system to transfer files to and fro, however.

The **rcp** command allows you to copy files and directories to and from a remote machine, provided you have the proper permissions (the same as the permissions required for the **rlogin** command, outlined in the previous section).

For instance: The following command line would copy the file **report.1995** from your home directory to a remote machine named *klingon*, into its **/home/reports** directory:

```
$ rcp /home/reports/report.1995 klingon:/home/reports
```

This method leaves the file with the same name. However, you could specify a new filename:

```
$ rcp /home/reports/report.1995 klingon:/home/reports/report
```

The same syntax can be applied to the process of copying from the remote system to your own. The following copies **report.1995** to your own home directory:

```
$ rcp klingon:/home/reports/report.1995 $HOME
```

The *-r* option copies entire subdirectories:

```
$ rcp-r klingon:/home/reports $HOME
```

The **rcp** command is summarized in Table 8.8.

TABLE 8.8 THE COMMAND REFERENCE FOR THE RCP COMMAND

rcp *options source target*

PURPOSE

The **rcp** copies files to and from remote systems. This command assumes that you have permissions in the target directory.

To name remote files, use *hostname:filename*.

OPTIONS

-**p**   Preserves the permissions of the source file.

-**r**   Recursively copy each subdirectory.

rsh *options hostname command*

PURPOSE

The **rsh** Starts a remote shell on a remote machine, executing a command on the remote machine.

On some systems, **rsh** refers to the *restricted* shell. The remote shell then is called **remsh**.

OPTIONS

-**l** *user*   Logs in *user* to the remote machine.

-**n**   Diverts input to **/dev/null**, which can be useful when troubleshooting.

▼

This Chapter in Review

▲   UNIX features a number of commands for communicating with other network users.

▲   Before you communicate with another networked user, you need to know who else is logged on the network. You can do so with the **who** and **rwho** commands.

▲   If you want to know more about a networked user, you can use the **finger** command to access a variety of information, such as the user's name and telephone number.

▲   The **write** command sends a message to another user logged on the network.

▲   The **talk** command allows you to carry on an interactive chat with another network user.

▲   To prevent others from requesting that you chat with them via **write** or **talk**, use the **mesg** command.

▲   The Berkeley Remote commands allow you to send files to and from remote systems networked to your own system. To work, you must have the proper permissions set up on both the remote and local UNIX systems.

▲   The **rlogin** command allows you to login a remote system and to run commands on that remote system. Typically, the commands and the directories are restricted.

▲   The **rcp** command copies files to and from a remote system.

▪ CHAPTER NINE ▪
The Internet

The Internet is riding the crest of an amazing wave of popularity in both the computer world and pop culture as a whole. Many of the more important and groundbreaking Internet tools, such as **mosaic**, were first designed for the UNIX world. In addition, many of the important resources that make up the Internet have their roots in the UNIX world. Topics in this chapter include:

▲ The future development of the Internet.

▲ Netsurfing the old way.

▲ Using **ftp.**

▲ Logging on a remote system via anonymous **ftp.**

▲ Using **telnet.**

▲ Using the **uncompress** and **unpack** commands.

▲ Using **archie** to find files at **ftp** sites.

▲ Using **gopher** to enter the world of **gopher** databases.

▲ Using the World Wide Web.

▲ Accessing the WWW with browsers, including **mosaic.**

▲ Searching the 'Net with WAIS.

▼

The Internet: A Cultural Revolution

It's impossible to wander through the popular media without running across metaphorical references to the Internet. From *Newsweek* to *Wired*, the Internet is one of the wonders of the late 20th century, and a roadmap for the communications of the 21st century.

Whether or not this is overkill is a matter for debate, of course. The Internet isn't as easy to access as most Internet geeks would have you believe, and the much-touted information on the Internet sometimes doesn't match the hype. Still, there's no doubt that the Internet can be a useful tool in a quest for obscure information; it's up to you do decide whether to put the time into such a quest.

You'vre already been exposed to two portions of what's typically included under the Internet umbrella: electronic mail and the Usenet. Up to this point in time, these two elements are really what have driven interest in the Internet—electronic mail is an amazing, handy capability, while the Usenet can be a very useful resource.

But the future clearly belongs to up-and-coming Internet tools like Gopher, Mosaic, and the World Wide Web. These are the tools that allow vast amounts of digitized data to be collected and catalogued—and, perhaps most importantly, organized in such a way that it can be easily found by computer users like yourself. One of the biggest problems with the Internet in the past has been the lack of organization when it came to information—neat things may have been available on the Internet, but few people knew how to access them.

This chapter covers the eerily suburbanlike sprawl that makes up the Internet, as well as the major Internet tools that run under the UNIX operating system. Not all of these tools will be installed on your system, of course; Internet connectivity is determined by your system administrator (who you should have a healthy working relationship with by now), and the exact tools used on the Internet will also be determined by your system administrator. This is by no means a complete guide to the Internet; over 100 books have been written about the Internet, and you're encouraged to go to Appendix A for a list of recommended works.

▼

Netsurfing the Old Way

Even though the Internet is a relatively new phenomenon in the cultural *Zeitgeist*, the UNIX operating system has long supported tools that allowed you to move files from one computer to another— or even login a remote computer as if it was in your own building or office.

These UNIX tools are still quite useful. And while some newer Internet users may pooh-pooh them as relics from the past, these older tools still are at the center of most serious Internet netsurfing.

Ftp

The **ftp** command connects you to any other computer on the Internet.

These computers may or not be using the UNIX operating system, but from your viewpoint it really doesn't matter. What's important is that both machines can use the **ftp** command.

Ftp stands for file transfer protocol. It is interactive software, which means it asks you for information at specific times. To run **ftp**, you type it on a command line:

```
$ ftp
ftp>
```

As do many other UNIX commands, the **ftp** command features its own prompt, letting you know that it is in change of the computing session. To get a list of available commands, use a question mark (**?**) at an **ftp** prompt:

```
$ ftp> ?
```

You also can establish a direct connection to a machine either by specifying the machine's name when you begin an **ftp** session:

```
$ ftp machinename
```

where *machinename* represents the name of the remote machine. You can also use the **open** command after starting an **ftp** session:

```
ftp> open
(to) machinename
Connected to machinename
```

where *machinename* refers to the remote Internet-connected computer.

Once you're logged in another machine, you can use UNIX commands to go through the remote system's filesystem (though there may be limitations on exactly what commands you can use; typically, you can only use navigational commands like **cd** and downloading comments).

Anonymous ftp

Under most circumstances, you need an account set up on a remote machine when you use the **ftp** command. This is especially true when you deal with the commercial world. Since it's impractical to set up an account for every user in a high-traffic situation, the practice of *anonymous ftp* evolved. Instead of having an account on the remote machine, you can login the remote machine as **anonymous**. Your privileges on the machine are extremely limited—you're allowed mainly to upload and download files from a specific directory, and that's about it—but this setup works very well.

To use anonymous ftp, you'd initiate an **ftp** session in the normal way. The difference is that you'd enter *anonymous* as your name, with your electronic-mail address (referred to as your *ident*) as your password:

```
ftp> open
(to) kevin.kevinmn.com
Connected to kevin.kevinmn.com
Name (kevin.kevinmn.com): anonymous
220 Guest login ok, send ident as password.
Password: kreichard@mcimail.com
230 Guest login ok, access restrictions apply.
```

From there you'd use the regular **ftp** commands.

Let's say you know through various sources that a really cool UNIX game is stored on the machine named *kevin.kevinmn.com* (no, this isn't a real machine) in the directory named /**games**. You also know that the name of the file is **deathrow.Z**.

You would then use the following command line to connect to the machine named *kevin.kevinmn.com*:

```
$ ftp kevin.kevinmn.com
```

If the connection goes through, you'll get a message saying so, along with a login prompt. Enter *anonymous* as your name:

```
Name (kevin.kevinmn.com): anonymous
```

and then enter your full username as the password:

```
220 Guest login ok, send ident as password.
Password: kreichard@mcimail.com
```

From there you can use the remote machine as if you were using the UNIX box in your own company. To make sure that the file you want is present, you can use the **ls** command as you would if you were looking for information on your own system. You can use **cd** to maneuver through a directory structure like the structure on your own UNIX system (that is, directories and subdirectories). In addition, you'll have access to additional **ftp** commands, as listed in Table 9.1. Don't worry about doing damage when you're logged on the remote computer; you can't do any harm, and the remote system is set up so that you can't accidentally erase any important files.

TABLE 9.1 COMMAND REFERENCE FOR THE FTP COMMAND

COMMAND	PURPOSE
? command	Displays help for specified *command.*
ascii	Sets transfer mode to ASCII (text) format.
bell	Creates a sound (usually a beep) after a file is transferred.
binary	Sets transfer mode to binary format.

TABLE 9.1 CONTINUED

bye or **quit**	Ends ftp session and ends the **ftp** program.
cdup	Changes the current directory to one level up on the directory hierarchy; same as **cd ...**
close	Ends ftp session with the remote machine, but continues the **ftp** command on the local machine.
delete *filename*	Removes *filename* from remote directory.
dir *directory filename*	Returns the contents of the specified *directory*; resulting information is stored in *filename*.
disconnect	Ends ftp session and **ftp** program.
get *file1 file2* or **recv** *file1 file2*	Gets *file1* from the remote machine and stores it under the filename *file2*; if *file2* is not specified, the *file1* name will be retained.
help *command*	Displays information about specified *command*; displays general help information if no *command* is specified.
mdelete *filename*(s)	Deletes *filename(s)* on the remote machine.
mdir *filename*(s)	Returns directory for multiple, specified *filename(s)*.
mget *filename*(s)	Gets the specified multiple *filename(s)* from the remote machine.
mput *filename*(s)	Puts the specified *filename(s)* on the remote machine.

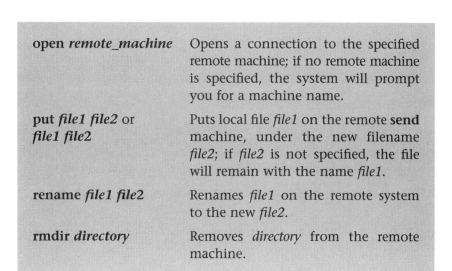

open *remote_machine*	Opens a connection to the specified remote machine; if no remote machine is specified, the system will prompt you for a machine name.
put *file1 file2* or *file1 file2*	Puts local file *file1* on the remote **send** machine, under the new filename *file2*; if *file2* is not specified, the file will remain with the name *file1*.
rename *file1 file2*	Renames *file1* on the remote system to the new *file2*.
rmdir *directory*	Removes *directory* from the remote machine.

By looking at the contents of the current directory, you know that **deathrow.Z** is in the current directory. (Most anonymous ftp sites are set up so that the most popular files are immediately accessible, without the need to search through many directories and subdirectories.) Before you do so, you need to make sure that the **ftp** command is prepared to transfer a file like this.

The .Z tells us that the file in question is a **compressed** file. Very often, larger files will be compressed so that the time needed to transfer them is minimized. How do you know that files are compressed? They end either with **.Z** or **.z**. UNIX files are compressed with two different commands: **compress** and **pack**. Files compressed with the **compress** command end with **.Z**, while files compressed with the **pack** command end with **.z**. You'll be constantly running across compressed files as you expand your Internet usage.

The commands to uncompress these files will depend on the command used to compress the files. To uncompress files compressed with the **compress** command (that is, ending with .Z), use the **uncompress** command (as shown in Table 9.2). To uncompress files compressed with the **pack** command (that is, ending with .z), use the **unpack** command (as shown in Table 9.3).

TABLE 9.2 COMMAND REFERENCE FOR THE UNCOMPRESS COMMAND

uncompress *option file(s)*

PURPOSE

The **uncompress** command does exactly what the name says: uncompresses a compressed file. These files usually have a name ending in **.Z**. When used, the newly compressed files will replace the original compressed file.

OPTION

-c   Uncompress without changing original *file(s)*.

TABLE 9.3 COMMAND REFERENCE FOR THE UNPACK COMMAND

unpack *file(s)*

PURPOSE

The **unpack** command unpacks a file shrunk with the **pack** commands. These files usually end with **.z**.

OPTIONS

None.

Anyway, to get to the reason for explaining compressed files: If a file is compressed, you must make sure the **ftp** command knows this. Since the compressed file is a binary file, you must tell this to the **ftp** command with the following command:

```
ftp> binary
```

Once you've done that, you can now grab the **deathrow.Z** file with the following command:

```
ftp> get deathrow.Z
```

When the file is transferring, there's no prompt, and the system won't accept your keystrokes. After the file has been transferred to your system, the system will tell you so in this manner:

```
Transfer complete
```

When you're done transferring files, use **bye** or **quit** to end the **ftp** command:

```
ftp> bye
```

Using the Telnet Command

The **telnet** command is one of the grand old warriors of the UNIX operating system.

Though seemingly shadowed by flashier and newer Internet tools, the **telnet** command in fact is still a useful and sometimes essential tools for any serious Internet usage.

The **telnet** command allows you to login a remote UNIX machine somewhere on the Internet. In some cases, you can run a command directly from that machine and display the results on your terminal, while in other cases you're limited to a specific program on the remote machine. You need only to know the address of the machine, such as *archie.rutgers.edu*. You can either open **telnet** and then specify the machine to connect to:

```
$ telnet
telnet> open archie.rutgers.edu
```

or you can connect to this machine directly from the command line:

```
$ telnet archie.rutgers.edu
Trying 128.6.18.15
Connected

SunOS UNIX (dorm.rutgers.edu)

login:
```

You'll then enter a password. If you're dealing with a system connected in some way to your corporation, you'll need a password. If you're connecting to a public Internet resource—which is the case here—you'll be given a public password (in this case, the password is *archie*).

▲ L E A R N   M O R E   A B O U T ▲

There are many public Internet resources, such as **gopher** and WAIS, that are accessible via the **telnet** command. You'll learn about these resources during the course of this chapter.

You would then use the remote machine as if it was a machine within your own building or corporation. Typically—especially with public Internet machines—you'll be limited to a very specific program, such as the **archie** program outlined in this example and elsewhere in this chapter. Each remote connection is different.

The **telnet** command is summarized in Table 9.4.

TABLE 9.4 COMMAND REFERENCE FOR THE TELNET COMMAND

telnet *system port*

PURPOSE

The **telnet** command logs you into a remote system using the TELNET protocol. After you login the remote system, your prompt will change to the **telnet** prompt (telnet>), from which you can enter TELNET commands. **telnet** also supports an input mode, where you can enter commands directly on the remote system. Use the escape character (**Ctrl-]** or ^, depending on your system setup) to switch between the two modes.

OPTIONS

system	Name of remote system or its network address.
port	Optional port identification.

ONLINE	COMMANDS
close	Ends remote session and exit the program.
display *values*	Displays **set** and **toggle** values.
mode *mode*	Changes mode to **character** or **line**.
open *system*	Opens connection to *system*.
quit	Ends remote session and exits the program.
send *chars*	Sends special characters to the remote system:

ao	abort output
ayt	are you there?
brk	break
ec	erase character
el	erase line
escape	Escape
ga	go ahead
ip	interrupt process
nop	no operation
synch	synch
?	help for **send** command

set value	Sets one of the following values:

echo	Local echo on or off
eof	end of file
erase	erase character
escape	new Escape character
flushoutput	flush output
interrupt	interrupt process
kill	erase line
quit	break

status	Displays status.
toggle *values*	Changes one of the following values:

autoflush	send interrupt or quit to remote system
autosynch	synch after **interrupt** or **quit**
crmod	convert **CR** to **CR LF**

TABLE 9.4 CONTINUED

	debug	debugging mode
	localchars	convert local commands to remote control
	netdata	covert hexadecimal display of network data
	options	protocol processing
	?	display settings
z	Suspends **telnet.**	
?	Displays summary of online commands.	

Netsurfing the New Way

As the Internet expanded beyond all reasonable expectations, users discovered that finding useful on the Internet could be next to impossible, unless one spent hours and hours sifting through remote systems and obscure directories. As a result, some forward-looking Internet devotees created some essential tools for cataloguing the vast resources of the Internet.

Archie

A product of McGill University in Toronto, Canada, **archie** is an attempt to organize the vast offerings of the Internet into a form that can be easily searched. This is not as straightforward a proposition as it might seem—the Internet is already vast and sprawling, and one of the major problems with it is the difficulty for users lacking degrees in computer science to actually find what they need on the 'Net. **Archie** is an attempt to change this. While **archie** works fairly well within the parameters of its mission, using it still can be somewhat of a challenge—so be prepared to spend some time with **archie** if you want to perform useful searches.

There are three ways you can use **archie** with your UNIX system:

▲ By having an **archie** program available on your system

▲ Through access to an **archie** server via the **telnet** command (which you've already covered in this chapter).

▲ Through electronic mail sent to an **archie** server

What exactly is an **archie** search? It's a search through FTP sites for a file somewhere on the Internet. Like any computer-based searches, you have some options before actually performing the search. For instance, you can look for a specific program and try to match its name exactly. Or else you can look for a string of characters that's part of a longer filename. You can tell the **archie** server to return the characters with the same case as in your search string, or else you can tell **archie** to ignore case.

All three methods outlined above have the same ultimate goal: to perform a search on an **archie** server. They differ in the details, however, so all three methods will be covered individually.

Using Archie on Your System

Most larger systems that rely on **archie** for daily work will have an **archie** command installed, which works like any other UNIX command.

The **archie** command sets up a connection to an **archie** server somewhere on the 'Net, performs the search on the remote **archie** server, and then ships the results back to you. Since the **archie** command performs most of the work (as opposed to connecting to an **archie** server via telnet or electronic mail), this is the easiest way to perform an **archie** search. The **archie** command is summarized in Table 9.5.

You may have an X Window System version of **archie**, called **xarchie**, installed on your system. This version makes the search process via **archie** somewhat easier. Its usage differs from the procedures outlined here, but the general principles remain the same.

TABLE 9.5 COMMAND REFERENCE FOR THE ARCHIE COMMAND.

archie *options string*

PURPOSE

The **archie** command is used to search for a text string among filenames listed with an **archie** server elsewhere on the Internet.

OPTIONS

-c	Searches for strings as part of a larger string, with an exact case match.
-e	Searches for a filename exactly matching your search string.
-h	Searches on a specified **archie** server, instead of the default **archie** server.
-l	Returns the results of the search one line at a time.
-L	Returns list of known **archie** servers.
-m*num*	Limits the number of search returns to *num*.
-o *file*	Sends the results of the search to *file*.
-s	Searches for strings as part of a larger string, without an exact case match.
-t	Returns the results of the search by time and date.

There's some variance as to exactly what **archie** searches for from server to server. Many of the public **archie** servers, such as *archie.internic.net* or *archie.unl.edu*, will look for a search string that's part of a larger string. Therefore, if you want to look for a specific string and nothing more, it's best to use **archie** with the *-e* option, telling it to look for *exactly* the specified string:

```
$ archie -e gcc
```

This command line tells **archie** to look for the **gcc** filename, but not any other filenames that contain *gcc* somewhere in the filename.

The **archie** command then performs a search on an **archie** server and then returns the results of the search to you:

```
Host harpo.seas.ucla.edu     (128.97.2.211)
Last updated 09:17 15 Aug 1994

   Location: /mnt/fs01
      DIRECTORY  dr-xr-xr-x  512 bytes  01:00 26 Feb 1993  gcc

   Location: /pub
      FILE  -rwxrwxrwx  15 bytes  01:00 27 Mar 1993  gcc
Host jhunix.hcf.jhu.edu  (128.220.2.5)
Last updated 08:50 15 Aug 1994

   Location:
/pub/public_domain_software/386BSD/source_tree/usr.bin_
      DIRECTORY  drwxr-xr-x  512 bytes  01:00  1 Jan 1994  gcc

   Location: /pub/public_domain_software/bsd-sources/usr.bin_
      DIRECTORY  dr-xr-xr-x  512 bytes  01:00 30 Nov 1993  gcc

Host interviews.stanford.edu  (36.22.0.175)
Last updated 18:19  5 Aug 1994

   Location: /dist/2.6/g++
      DIRECTORY  drwxr-xr-x  3072 bytes  01:00  6 Feb 1990  gcc

Host karazm.math.uh.edu     (129.7.128.1)
Last updated 09:36  5 Aug 1994

   Location: /pub/Amiga/comp.sys.amiga.reviews/all
      FILE  -rwxrwxrwx  26 bytes  20:32  4 Mar 1994  gcc

   Location: /pub/Amiga/comp.sys.amiga.reviews/software/programmer
      FILE  -rw-r--r--  4069 bytes  20:32  4 Mar 1994  gcc
```

For space purposes, the entire list was truncated. Obviously, this **archie** search was a success, as **archie** displays some machines on the Internet storing **gcc**. One such listing was:

```
Host jaguar.cs.utah.edu  (155.99.212.101)
Last updated 10:32  3 Aug 1994

   Location: /dist/hpuxbin/bin
      FILE  -rwxr-xr-x  82428 bytes  23:29 18 Apr 1994  gcc
```

There's a host of information in this listing—enough information so that you could use anonymous FTP and grab the file from the host **jaguar.cs.utah.edu**. You're told the:

- ▲ Name of the host containing the files (**jaguar.cs.utah.edu**)
- ▲ Internet address of the host containing the files (**155.99.212.101**)
- ▲ Location on the host (**/dist/hpuxbin/bin**)
- ▲ Size of the file (**82428 bytes**)
- ▲ Name of the file (**gcc**)

There's also some other very useful information here, which you may not have picked up on immediately—but information that could save you a vast amount of time as you do your Internet searches.

Because filenames themselves can be highly undescriptive—even when using the longer filenames common in the UNIX world—you sometimes need to play detective and to try to divine as much information as possible from the server. In this case, you're obviously looking for a copy of the GNU C compiler, **gcc**, for use on your own system.

Take a closer look at the location on the host: **/dist/hpuxbin/bin**. Generally speaking, anything on a UNIX system—whether on the Internet or on your own UNIX system—stored within **bin** is going to be a binary file (in other words, it's a file that you can run). The *hpuxbin* is a reference to the HP-UX version of UNIX from Hewlett-Packard. Putting this all together, it's pretty clear that the **gcc** file stored on *jaguar.cs.utah.edu* is actually a version of **gcc** for HP-UX. If you're not using HP-UX, this version of **gcc** would be pretty worthless for you. But if you're using HP-UX, then this **gcc** is for you.

As mentioned, the results of the search for **gcc** were quite voluminous. There are two ways to manage this rush of information. You can either limit the number of matches with the *-m* option:

```
$ archie -e -m20 gcc
```

or you can merely redirect the results of the command to a file:

```
$ archie -e gcc > gccreturns
```

▼

Connecting to an Archie Server via Telnet

You don't need an **archie** server on your system to make use of **archie**. If you have access to **telnet**, you can connect to an **archie** server. There aren't many **archie** servers in the world open to everyone, and the ones that exist are frightfully busy, so don't abuse this privilege by spending hours and hours searching via **archie** for some obscure file you really don't need. Some useful North American **archie** servers are:

▲ *archie.sura.net* (Maryland)

▲ *archie.internix.net* (New Jersey)

▲ *archie.rutgers.edu* (New Jersey)

▲ *archie.unl.edu* (Nebraska)

▲ *archie.mcgill.edu* (Toronto)

▲ *archie.uqam.ca* (Canada)

Some useful international **archie** servers include:

▲ *archie.univie.ac.at* (Austria)

▲ *archie.doc.ic.ac.uk* (Great Britain)

▲ *archue.funet.fi* (Finland)

▲ *archie.au* (Australia)

▲ *archie.th-darmstadt.de* (Germany)

▲ *archie.sogang.ac.kr* (Korea)

▲ *archie.wide.ad.jp* (Japan)

 If possible, choose an **archie** site closest to you. You shouldn't be abusing the Internet and doing all of your **archie** searches on servers in Europe and Asia. Someone has to pay the long-distance international phone bill when this occurs.

The same goes for any other Internet activity, such as **ftp** or **telnet**.

Using an **archie** server isn't a big deal, but you do need to master the mechanics before you can get any work done. A typical **archie** server session is shown in Figure 9.1.

▼

```
SunOS UNIX (sifon)

login: archie

*************************************************************

   Welcome to the InterNIC Directory and Database Server

*************************************************************

# Bunyip Information Systems, 1993

# Terminal type set to `network 24 80'.
# `erase' character is `^?'.
# `search' (type string) has the value `sub'.
archie> find lynx
working...

Host ftp.sura.net   (128.167.254.179)
Last updated 07:32 18 Aug 1993

   Location: /pub/archie/sites/local
      FILE  -rw-rw-r—  1759 bytes  04:32 28 Apr 1993 lynx.ps.uci.edu.Z

Host cwaves.stfx.ca   (141.109.27.2)
Last updated 05:47 31 May 1993

   Location: /pub/c128/Utilities/Archive
      FILE:  -rw-r—r—  34816 bytes  07:46  9 Feb 1993 ult.lynx-XII-128
      FILE:   -rw-r—r—   32640 bytes  00:00 23 Apr 1992 ult.lynx.v17

Host ftp.germany.eu.net    (192.76.144.75)
Last updated 06:30 17 Aug 1993

   Location: /newsarchive/comp.sources.atari.st/column4
archie>
```

FIGURE 9.1 A typical archie session

Figure 9.1 illustrates the information that you need when you launch an **archie** session on a server. After you open the **telnet** session and specify the **archie** server, you're presented with an login prompt. You don't need a username or password; just type *archie* and hit the **Return** key.

▼

Some **archie** servers present information about the server and how it's configured; others throw an **archie** prompt at you, as in the following:

```
archie>
```

In Figure 9.1, the **archie** server conveniently informs us that the search variable is set for *sub*. This is the least rigorous of the possible settings for the search variable, as you'll see in Table 9.6.

TABLE 9.6 AVAILABLE SETTINGS FOR THE ARCHIE SEARCH VARIABLE

SETTING	RESULT
exact	Requires the string used with **find** or **prog** to exactly match the filename.
regex	Requires the string used with **find** or **prog** to be treated as a regular UNIX expression.
sub	Requires the string used with **find** or **prog** to appear somewhere in the filename.
subcase	Requires the string used with **find** or **prog** to appear somewhere in the filename in the exact case.

The settings listed in Table 9.6 are changed with a command to the **archie** server, some of which are shown in Table 9.5. There are many **archie** commands—more than those listed in Table 9.5—but you'll most often use only a few of them.

The commands used when you are connected to an **archie** server are different than the commands you use with an **archie** command installed on your own system.

Table 9.7 lists the available commands when connected to an **archie** server.

**TABLE 9.7 AVAILABLE COMMANDS
WHEN CONNECTED TO AN ARCHIE SERVER**

COMMAND	RESULT
exit	Quits the connection to the **archie** server.
find *string*	Searches the database for *string*. (The same as **prog**.)
help or ?	Displays a list of available commands.
help *command*	Displays information about a specific *command*.
prog *string*	Searches the database for *string*. (The same as **find**.)
servers	Displays list of servers archived by this **archie** server and when they were last checked for new files.
set search exact	Searches the database for an exact string.
set search sub	Searches the database to look for *string* as a portion of the whole filename.
show	Displays all of the variables associated with **archie**.
whatis *string*	Searches a separate database of software descriptions for *string*.

Going back to Figure 9.1: Because the search variable was already set to *sub*, there was no reason to change, so a search was conducted immediately. In this particular case, the search was for the string *lynx*, in the hopes of finding the program **lynx**, a tool for browsing the Internet through VT100 terminals.

There's another tool on a typical **archie** server that you may find useful: the **whatis** command. Because the filenames of many programs can be on the obscure side, some ambitious **archie** organizers got together and decided to associated descriptive keywords with their filenames. The **whatis** command allows you to search through these keywords, in case you don't know the exact filename of something you're looking for, or are looking for a type of software rather than a specific title. The command then gives you a description of the files that match your query, which you can then search for using the **prog** or **find** commands. The following is a rather simplistic use of the **whatis** command:

```
archie> whatis gcc
gcc   The GNU C compiler
```

You'll then be presented with hosts that contain this software.

If there are many servers listed, you may find it easier to have **archie** send back the results of the search via electronic mail. (This is different than initiating the search via electronic mail, which is covered in the next section.) To do this, perform your search as described above. When finished, give the following command to **archie**:

```
archie> mail
```

Using Archie Via Electronic Mail

If you have the name of an **archie** server, you can also send it electronic mail to get the results of an **archie** search. To do so, use **mail**, **mailx**, or your favorite mail package (by this time you should be intimately familiar with your favorite mail readers) and compose a mail message to the **archie** server. Within the message, you should insert the **archie** commands you want the machine to run. You can combine multiple searches within a mail message.

The following shows a typical mail message:

```
$ mail archie@archie.unl.edu
Subject: Archie Search
prog gcc
```

If you're lucky, within a matter of hours you'll have a response to your query. Figure 9.2 shows a typical response to a mail query to an **archie** server.

```
Return-Path: <archie-errors@crcnis2.unl.edu>
To: <reichard@MR.Net>
From:  (Archie Server)archie-errors@crcnis2.unl.edu
Reply-To:  (Archie Server)archie-errors@crcnis2.unl.edu
Date: Mon, 5 Sep 94 0:46 GMT
Subject: archie [prog gcc] part 1 of 1

>> path <reichard@MR.Net>

>> prog gcc
# Search type: exact.
Host interviews.stanford.edu  (36.22.0.175)
Last updated 18:19  5 Aug 1994

   Location: /dist/2.6/g++
      DIRECTORY  drwxr-xr-x  3072 bytes  01:00  6 Feb 1990  gcc
Host en.ecn.purdue.edu  (128.46.149.59)
Last updated 13:05  3 Aug 1994

   Location: /
      DIRECTORY  drwxr-xr-x  1024 bytes  00:00 13 Jul 1993  gcc

Host leland.stanford.edu  (36.21.0.69)
Last updated 11:31  3 Aug 1994

   Location: /pub/cs240a/lib/bin
      FILE  -rwxr-xr-x  114688 bytes  01:00  6 Jan 1994  gcc

Host jaguar.cs.utah.edu  (155.99.212.101)
Last updated 10:32  3 Aug 1994

   Location: /dist/hpuxbin/bin
      FILE  -rwxr-xr-x  82428 bytes 23:29 18 Apr 1994  gcc

Host gatekeeper.dec.com  (16.1.0.2)
Last updated 01:31  4 Jul 1994

   Location: /contrib/.mips-ultrix/bin
      FILE  -rwxr-xr-x  61440 bytes  00:00  8 Oct 1992  gcc

   Location: /contrib/.mips-ultrix/lib/gcc-lib/mips-dec-ultrix4.2/2.2.2
      FILE  -rwxr-xr-x  114304 bytes  00:00  1 Aug 1992  gcc
```

▼

```
[[[LOTS OF HOSTS DELETED FOR SPACE]]]
>> quit
```

FIGURE 9.2 A mail response from an archie server

The query in Figure 9.2 generated many, many hosts that had **gcc** somewhere on them. If you send queries to an **archie** server and you expect that they might generate a long list of matches, you'll want to tell the **archie** server to send you the results of the commands in a compressed file. To do so, add a line to the end of your e-mail message, as in the following example:

```
$ mail archie@archie.unl.edu
Subject: Archie Search
prog gcc
compress
```

When the e-mail returns, a file will be attached to it, and you'll need to use the uncompress command to **uncompress** it.

Gopher

One of the first efforts to harnass the immense power of the Internet came at the University of Minnesota, where officials were faced with the problem of cataloguing useful information that could be accessed by the more than 30,000 University of Minnesota students. The solution was **gopher** (a pun on the mascot of the U of M, the Golden Gophers), which would go over a network and connect to a remote server. Since **gopher** worked so well at the University of Minnesota, the source code was freely distributed across the Internet. That lead to a host of **gopher** servers across the world, as well as a host of **gopher** clients created for a variety of operating systems.

Today, **gopher** servers are everywhere, or so it seems. You can read Usenet news from a **gopher** in Great Britain. You can grab software stored on any number of **gopher** servers. A whole host of offerings can be accessed via a **gopher** menu called *Gopher Jewels*. Software can be grabbed just by selecting from a list of available titles. The many functions of a **gopher** lessen the need for **ftp** or **telnet** sessions; if a file is linked to a **gopher** server, it can be downloaded within the parameters of the current **gopher** session.

The best way to illustrate **gopher** is to run through a few examples. Don't worry if the examples in this section don't match the specifics on your **gopher** program. Each **gopher** is configured a little bit differently. For instance, when **gopher** is launched, it immediately connects to a home **gopher** server. This home server may reside on your corporate computing environment, or it may reside elsewhere on the Internet. For instance, the examples used in this chapter will revolve around the home server at the **gopher** run by the Minnesota Regional Network (MRNet), a service provider in Minneapolis, Minnesota, as well as **gopher** servers connected with the University of Minnesota. Chances are pretty good, however, that your home servers won't be connected with MRNet or the University of Minnesota. Follow this section and note the actions taken to accomplish the task, not the specific menus choices outlined.

When you login a **gopher** via **telnet**, you'll be presented with a screen that looks like the following:

```
* * *   University of Minnesota * * *
    * *   Public Gopher Access   * *
Type 'gopher' at the login prompt
AIX Version 3
(C) Copyrigh
ts by IBM and by others 1982, 1993.
login: gopher
```

At this point, you can just enter *gopher* as the login name. On a public **gopher** server, you don't need to enter a password or username.

After the login is accepted, you'll be presented something like the following:

```
This machine is a public gopher client.

You are sharing this machine with many other people from all
around the Internet.

To get better performance we recommend that you install a
gopher client on your own machine.  Gopher clients are
available for Unix, Macintosh, DOS, OS/2, VMS, CMS, MVS,
Amiga, and many others

You can get these clients via anonymous ftp from
boombox.micro.umn.edu in the directory /pub/gopher

The Gopher Team thanks you!
```

```
Last unsuccessful login: Mon Aug 15 17;42:30 CDT 1994 on pts/0
from arcwelder.micro.umn.edu
Last login: Mon Sep 5 11:36:22 CDT on pts/9 from lobby.ti.com
TERM = (vt100) _
```

At this point, you'll be presented with a list of options, such as further options and information about this particular **gopher** server.

Connecting directly to a public **gopher**, however, isn't considered good form for extended usage. Instead, you really should be using **gopher** clients on your own system. (If there's no **gopher** software on your system, see your system administrator.) There are **gopher** clients for virtually every operating system, and some have chosen to make subtle changes to **gopher**—creating a wealth of implementations to choose from. For UNIX users, there are text-based versions as well as X Window System versions.

Using Gopher

Every **gopher** version works in basically the same way, however. You begin **gopher** either on the command line:

```
$ gopher
```

or by clicking on a **gopher** icon. If you want to connect to a specific **gopher** server other than the default **gopher** server, you can specify it on the command line:

▼

```
$ gopher boombox.micro.umn.edu
```

Your **gopher** client then connects to a **gopher** server, either on your own system or across the 'Net. After you're connected to the **gopher** server, you're presented with a list of options. For instance, when connecting to **gopher.mr.net**, the following options are displayed in some fashion:

```
Minnesota Regional Network Gopher Hotel
Minnesota Regional Network
Object Database Management Group (gopher.odmg.org. 2073)
Minnesota Datametrics Corporation (gopher.mndata.com, 2074)
Jostens Incorporated (gopher.jostens.com, 2071)
```

We say *in some fashion* because the exact look and feel will depend on your version of **gopher**. With a graphical version, you'll see the above augmented by fancy fonts and little graphics indicating whether the line is a document or a directory. With a nongraphical version, you'll have numerals at the beginning of the lines (1, 2, 3, et al) and slashes (/) indicating directories.

Perhaps the best thing about **gopher** is that someone has already gone to a lot of work to make your searches go more smoothly. When you choose an item from a list, the **gopher** server already contains information about the item, and it makes the connection automatically. For instance, in our previous example from MRNet, there are three **gophers** listed with separate addresses. They may or not reside on the same machine—but as far as you're concerned, it doesn't matter. The **gopher** server will do the work of moving to the next set of menu choices. Because of this interlinking of **gopher** resources, you may end up connecting with **gophers** across the country, and perhaps the world, as you go in search of information.

If you're new to **gopher** and want an overview of the vast resources collected on **gopher** databases, you may want to check out Gopher Jewels, a menu item that's found on many larger **gopher** servers. Actually maintained at **cwis.usc.edu** (a **gopher** at the University of Southern California), but referenced to by many **gopher** servers (the good ones, at least), Gopher Jewels is a listing of essential and note-worthy **gopher** resources, as is written in the information statement:

Gopher Jewels offers a unique approach to gopher subject
tree design and content. It is an alternative to the more
traditional subject tree design. Although many of the features,
individually, are not new the combined set represents the
best features found on sites around the world. We offer
solutions to navigating information by subject as an experiment
in the evolution of information cataloging. Our focus is
on locating information by subject and does not attempt to
address the quality of the information we point to.

Gopher Jewels offers the following:
— Over 2,000 pointers to information by category
— Jughead search of all menus in Gopher Jewels
— The option to jump up one menu level from any directory
— The option to jump to the top menu from any directory
— Gopher Tips help documents
— Gopher Jewels list archives
— Gopher Jewels - Talk list archives
— Other gopher related archives
— Help and archives searchable (WAIS)

When you choose the Gopher Tools menu choice, you'll see a listing
like the following:

```
—>1.  GOPHER JEWELS Information and Help/
   2.  Community, Global and Environmental/
   3.  Education, Social Sciences, Arts & Humanities/
   4.  Economics, Business and Store Fronts/
   5.  Engineering and Industrial Applications/
   6.  Government/
   7.  Health, Medical, and Disability/
   8.  nternet and Computer Related Resources/
   9.  Law/
  10.  Library, Reference, and News/
  11.  Miscellaneous Items/
  12.  Natural Sciences including Mathematics/
  13.  Personal Development and Recreation/
  14.  Research, Technology Transfer and Grants Opportunities/
  15.  Search Gopher Jewels Menus by Key Word(s)

Press ? for help, q to quit, u to go up   Page 1/1
```

▼

With **gopher**, there are directories and there are resources. In theory, there should be a resource buried somewhere in a pile of directories, but sometimes you must wade through many, many directories to get at a resource.

With this list, you can tell which lines are directories, as they end with a slash (/). You can also tell which lines are resources—they're the ones without slashes.

Your menu may not look exactly like the previous example. For instance, if you're working with a graphical version of **gopher**, there won't be any numbers at the beginning of a line or slashes at the end of a line. Instead, there will be little file-folder icons representing directories at the beginning of lines, and a little magnifying glass in front of the last line of the listing, indicating that a search is performed by the menu choice. (Resources can have several representational icons—files don't use magnifying-glass icons, for instance.)

In this case, you'd use the keyboard's cursor keys (the four keys with arrows on them) to move up and down the menu. When the arrow on the left side of the menu is next to the menu item you want to choose, press the **Return** key. Or, more simply, you could type the number of the menu item, followed by the **Return** key.

Perhaps simplest of all—if you're using a graphical interface, you can move the cursor over the line and click.

If you were to choose *13. Personal Development and Recreation*, you'd be placed yet in another set of menus and directories:

```
->1.  Employment Opportunities and Resume Postings/
   2.  Fun Stuff & Multimedia/
   3.  Museums, Exhibits and Special Collections/
   4.  Travel Information/
```

You can see why people claim that it's easy to get lost in cyberspace—when you have to wade through four or five sets of menus to find a nugget of usable information, you stand a pretty good chance of being confused by the proceedings.

Some Popular Gopher Resources

There's not much more to using **gopher**. Indeed, you'll learn more by poking around cyberspace and seeing what you find. It's actually pretty easy to connect to remote **gophers** around the world—most larger **gopher** servers contain lists of all the known **gopher** servers in the world, and these lists are typically organized either as one huge list or broken into alphabetical or regional lists.

Many useful and fun resources have been placed on **gopher** servers. Some are listed in Table 9.8.

TABLE 9.8 POPULAR GOPHER SERVERS

SERVER	CONTENT
basun.sunet.se	Swedish-language **gopher**; answers the immortal question, *Var är Gopher?*
boombox.micro.umn.edu	The repository for **gopher** software.
envirolink.org	Environmental information for activists and others concerned about the environment.
gopher.ic.ac.uk	A large collection of DOS and *Windows* software.
info-server.lanl.gov	Usenet news. (Be sure to use server port 4320 and selector *nntp*.)
internic.net	Information about the various services offered on the Internet.

TABLE 9.8 CONTINUED

nkosi.well.sf.ca	Service of the Whole Earth 'Lectronic Link (WELL), which includes articles from *Mondo 2000*, *Wired Magazine*, *Gnosis*, *Locus*, and *Whole Earth Review*; writings from the like of Bruce Sterling and William S. Burroughs; and links to a whole host of other **gopher** servers.
peg.cwis.uci.edu	A listing of government **gopher** servers.
wx.atmos.uiuc.edu	The University of Illinois Department of Atmospheric Sciences Weather Machine **gopher** server, which provides weather maps gathered from satellite data.

To learn more about **gopher** servers and to see periodic announcements about new **gopher** resources, you'll want to monitor the *comp.infosystems.gopher* and *alt.gopher* newsgroups.

Veronica

Of course, you don't need to know what exists on every **gopher** server on the Internet—keeping track of the contents of over 1,500 **gopher** servers might prove to be a daunting task. Instead, you can turn to a popular searching tool, **veronica** (named by its creators at the University of Nevada after the comic-book character, and not coincidentally a pun on **archie**), which will search through a database of offerings on **gopher** servers—a database that makes up gopherspace, in the Internet parlance.

You access **veronica** through a **gopher** server. Most larger **gopher** servers feature connections to a **veronica** server. The menu lines indicating such a link will look something like this:

```
14. Search GopherSpace at the InforMNs Veronica
```

Veronica isn't always the most reliable way to search for information. There are many **veronica** servers across the 'Net, and there are even more **gopher** servers—both being updated and changed every day. The example searches in this section were executed through the InforMN **veronica** server. Your **veronica** server may differ.

A **veronica** server isn't an exceptionally complex creature: You connect to it via a **gopher** server and tell it what to search for. For instance, you may want to see what Cajun recipes are available on the vast range of **gopher** servers. Entering *cajun* as a search term on the InforMN **veronica** server yields 64 responses, including the following resource:

```
14. cajun.sausage.paella (4K)
```

Choosing that menu item connects you to **cadadmin.cadlab.vt.edu** and displays a recipe for Cajun sausage paella.

Of course, not all of the 64 resources have to do with cooking— which leads us to a rule of Internet searching: Make your search terms as precise as possible. For instance, the search for *cajun* also yielded a small item surrounding a 1985 headline from a Minnesota newspaper (just which one isn't exactly clear—though it's probably the Minnesota *Daily*, the campus newspaper at the University of Minnesota), announcing that the Gophers are bound for "Cajun-country" after being invited to a football bowl game.

▼

Jughead

A smaller-scale version of **veronica** is **jughead** (yes, named for the comic-book character; originated at the University of Utah), which will perform searches on a regional level. There aren't too many **jughead** servers littering the outposts of cyberspace, mainly because someone must go to the work of setting up the **jughead** server to contain only items of a regional nature.

The World Wide Web

The World Wide Web, or WWW, is perhaps one of the most important computing efforts of the last 50 years. Created and overseen by CERN (the European Laboratory for Particle Physics), the WWW is an attempt to create a worldwide distributed hypermedia system. It's also why most Internet users are bullish on the future of the Internet as a useful and exciting way to distribute information around the world.

A *distributed hypermedia system?* In English, this means that Internet documents can contain links to other Internet documents. In this case, an Internet document can be a file on an FTP site (the sort of thing you used **archie** to search for earlier in this chapter), the contents of a Usenet newsgroup, the result of a WAIS search, or a **telnet** connection to another Internet-connected machine. In short, the format of the document shouldn't matter if you're on the WWW; you should be able to move between any Internet documents without having to use multiple tools to access them. And everything should be transparent to the user, who shouldn't have to care if a document is stored on an FTP site, a **gopher** server, or something else.

In addition, the design of WWW documents is unlike anything else on the Internet. Thanks to the assumption that most Internet browsers will contain some basic fonts, most WWW documents look more like "real" documents (as in something you would see in a book or magazine) than a page of text on a computer screen. In addition, most WWW browsers contain the ability to display graphics, which

▼

are sent in compressed form over the Internet and then uncompressed on your machine.

▲ **L E A R N   M O R E   A B O U T** ▲

You'll see some examples of attractive WWW graphics later in this chapter.

The best way to illustrate these WWW documents and links is to examine a typical WWW site on the Internet. Since coffee played a large role in the creation of this book, it's only fitting that Over The Coffee, a WWW site, be used as the example WWW site.

To get to a WWW site, you first need to have the document's Uniform Resource Locator, or URL. URLs come in a variety of formats, but they all look basically the same; the differences lie in the type of document that they represent. The range of URLs and their formats are summarized in Table 9.9.

TABLE 9.9 URL FORMATS AND THEIR MEANINGS, COURTESY OF THE WWW FAQ

FORMAT	REPRESENTS
file://wuarchive.wustl.edu/mirrors/ msdos/graphics/gifkit.zip	File at an FTP site.
ftp: //wuarchive.wustl.edu/mirrors	FTP site.
http:/info.cern.ch:80/default.html	WWW site.
news:alt.hypertext	Usenet newsgroup.
telnet://dra.com	**Telnet** connection to Internet-connected server.

The URL for Over The Coffee is *hhtp://www.infonet.net/showcase/coffee.* When you use this URL in your browser, you'll be connected to Over The Coffee site, as shown in Figure 9.3.

▼

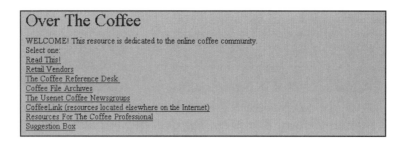

FIGURE 9.3 The opening page of the Over The Coffee WWW site

 The documents that you view from the WWW may not look exactly like Figure 9.3. (For example, the originating screen featured color—the underlined lines were also highlighted in blue.) There are a number of Internet browsers that allow you to view WWW documents, such as *Mosaic* (which will be covered later in this chapter), and they all work a little differently in terms of fonts and color support. In addition, some of the Internet browsers, such as *Lynx*, display only the text from a WWW page.

As far as WWW sites go, Over The Coffee is short and sweet, announcing its purpose and displaying a list of menu choices. Though it's not reflected in Figure 9.3, this WWW site represents menu choices in blue, in addition to the underlining. Depending on your WWW browser, you'll either click on the menu choice with a mouse or you'll use the cursor keys to move a cursor over the menu items you want to access. Selecting "Coffee File Archives," for instance, gets you the screen shown in Figure 9.4.

FIGURE 9.4 "Coffee File Archives" at Over The Coffee WWW site

▼

In this case, you've been linked to an FTP site, albeit one on the same machine containing Over The Coffee. How do you know it? When files and FTP sites are represented on a WWW document, the filenames are indicated by little pages (in this case, displayed next to **caffaq17.txt**), and the subdirectories are illustrated with little file folders. The path of the current directory is displayed at the top of the screen.

Another feature in Over The Coffee that illustrates the power of the WWW is the "The Usenet Coffee Newsgroups" menu choice, which takes you to a menu accessing the three coffee-related newsgroups, as shown in Figure 9.5. Selecting one of the three newsgroups will give you a listing of the articles in the newsgroup.

The Usenet Coffee-Related Newsgroups

Select A Usenet News Group:
alt.coffee
rec.food.drink.coffee
alt.drugs.caffeine

FIGURE 9.5 The Usenet newsgroups accessed through Over The Coffee

A more explicit link to other Internet resources is accessed by the menu choice "CoffeeLink" and shown in Figure 9.6.

Links To Other Coffee Resources On The Internet:

Cafe Mam (Organically grown Mexican coffee)
Capulin Coffee (Ash Creek Orchards)
Mothercity Coffee (Seattle Coffee Houses)
Caffeine Homepage (Matthew Loew)
FAQ: Caffeine's Frequently Asked Questions (Lopez-Ortiz)
The Trojan Room Coffee Machine (Cambridge, UK)

FIGURE 9.6 The gateway to other Internet coffee resources

Choosing "Mothercity Coffee" will get you the document shown in Figure 9.7.

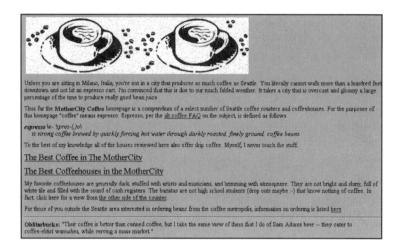

FIGURE 9.7 Mother City coffee—Seattle coffeehouses in all their glory

The important point here isn't to show the vast amount of coffee information available over the Internet. The thing to remember is that documents on the WWW are frequently linked to other documents on the WWW.

Finding Things on the WWW

As with the creators of **archie** and **veronica**, the WWW organizers have taken the time to catalogue the vast offerings of the WWW. CERN maintains the Virtual Library, which is a listing of resources, broken down into different categories. It can be found at:

```
http://info.cern.ch/hypertext/DataSources/bySubject/Overview.html
```

Getting on the WWW

Your system administrator needs to handle the details of getting your company connected to the World Wide Web. Generally speaking, the best method is through a direct connection to the Internet, which can then be accessed on your UNIX by a browser like *Viola*, *Mosaic*, or *Lynx*.

If you want to get a taste of the World Wide Web, however, you can use **telnet** to connect to a public WWW browser. These browsers are text-only and are designed to give you a look at the WWW; extended usage is highly discouraged, and to be honest you'll be frustrated in dealing with a limited (most allow you only to poke around the local WWW site, not other WWW sites) and frumpy entrance into the WWW. Public browsers in the United States include **www.cc.kans.edu** (a text-only browser that requires VT100 emulation), **fatty.law.cornell.edu** (New York), and **www.njit.edu** (at the New Jersey Institute of Technology; use a logname of *www*), while CERN (the originators and overseers of WWW) maintains a site at **info.cern.ch**. (Since it requires a connection to Switzerland, you shouldn't really use this site often.)

UNIX users have a wide variety of web browsers available:

▲ *NCSA Mosaic for the X Window System*

▲ *tkWWW Browser/Editor for X11* (written in the Tcl/Tk language)

▲ *MidasWWW* (runs under X)

▲ *Viola for X*

▲ *Chimera*

▲ *Lynx* (text only)

▲ *perlWWW* (a text-only browser written in the perl language)

▲ *Emacs* w3-mode (an *emacs* mode that allows browsing on the WWW)

Mosaic

The most popular of these browsers is *NCSA Mosaic for the X Window System* (which will be referred to for the remainder of this chapter as **mosaic**), from the National Center for Supercomputing Applications. Indeed, if there's one tool that has popularized the concept of the WWW, it's **mosaic**.

If you're using **mosaic**, you're probably already familiar with many of the resources listed in this chapter; after all, most of them, such as access to the CERN Virtual Library. You launch **mosaic** with the following command line:

```
$ mosaic
```

This takes you to a default URL, or *home page*, which you connect to every time you launch **mosaic**. If you want to connect to a different URL, you can use a command line like the following:

```
$ mosaic hhtp://www.infonet.net/showcase/coffee
```

In this case, a window appears on your screen, with the contents of Figure 9.3 (shown earlier in this chapter) within.

The best way to learn about **mosaic** is to play with it. There's little written documentation for **mosaic**; instead, you can access a ton of **mosaic** information through **mosaic** itself by choosing one of many help resources (found under the **Help** menu) that you download from the NCSA as needed. Using **mosaic** is not an exceptionally difficult task—really, all **mosaic** does is allow you to browse the Web—and after taking a few minutes to run down all your menu choices, you should have a good grasp on the things you can do with **mosaic**.

Searching the 'Net with WAIS

Some Internet users have access to a powerful searching tool called Wide Area Information Service, or WAIS. This is another attempt to catalogue the vast resources of the Internet into a format that can easily be accessed by anyone.

You can access WAIS through several means: Through WAIS software (which isn't yet in wide distribution among Internet users), through **telnet** connection to a public WAIS server, through Mosaic, or through **gopher**.

To do a **telnet** connection to a public WAIS server, you first need to know the name of the server. There aren't many yet, so your choices in the United States are limited to:

▲ **quake.think.com** (login as *wais*)

▲ **swais.cwis.uci.edu** (login as *swais*)

▲   **nnsc.nfs.net** (login as *wais*)

▲   **sunsite.unc.edu** (login as *swais*)

In addition, most larger **gopher** sites have access to a WAIS server, usually buried in some menu choice.

WAIS is designed to be accessible to anyone. When you're connected to a WAIS server, you can enter as many keywords as you like, and then the WAIS server conducts the search. The exact procedures now vary from WAIS server to WAIS server (the process on **quake.think.com** differs from the process on **sunsite.unc.edu**, for example), so you'll have to learn by doing in this case.

The Network of the Future

There's been a lot of blather in the media about the Internet serving as a roadmap for a future government information infrastructure. Don't bet on it—the Internet is already showing some signs of weakness, as the needs of new users (especially businesses who want to exploit the Internet for commercial gain) are clashing with the wishes of the Internet pioneers. The corporations who pay the freight for the Internet— the firms that maintain hundreds of long-distance and international phone connections—are indicating that they are tired of subsidizing the hundred of thousands of users who get a free connection through a college or university. The National Science Foundation, at the time this book was written, had withdrawn funding for the Internet and announced that private industry should be willing to carry on the costs of the Internet—a move that sent shock waves through the Internet infrastructure, as many of the freeloaders have been warned that their days of free passage have ended.

Predictably enough, these users have responded with fear and loathing, arguing that the Internet should be subsidized by the government as an essential part of modern living. Their cries have been met mostly by silence, as private industry has gone ahead and instituted new pricing structures for universities, colleges, and non-profits—institutions weaned and seduced by low-cost access. The clash between competing interests won't disappear, either, as the Internet is only at the beginning of a difficult transition. Don't be surprised if the Internet, as we know it today, doesn't exist by the millennium.

In the short term, however, the Internet is proving to be easier and easier to use. UNIX folks tend to think in terms of tools—small, specialized commands that perform a limited range of functions; hence, **ftp**, **telnet**, **gopher**, **archie**, and a range of other Internet commands.

But the rest of the world doesn't have this mindset, and we're on the edge of a more enlightened era, when a UNIX user can use a single tool to access the many offerings of the Internet. *NCSA Mosaic* is one step in that direction, allowing you to access **gopher** servers as well as HTML pages—but if you want to read your mail or Usenet newsgroups, you still need a separate UNIX tool. Commercial offerings, from the likes of Spyglass and Spry, extend the idea of a browser further and are incorporating essential functions under one software umbrella. (Interestingly enough, the only tool that allows you to launch **ftp** and **telnet** sessions, send mail, and read linked Usenet newsgroups is available for the Microsoft *Windows* environment—*Cello*. UNIX users would do well to take a look at *Cello* as a blueprint for Internet browsers.)

At the moment, the medium does matter when looking for information on the Internet. In the future, the Internet will appear as a seamless mass of data, with a single browsing tool that will allow *any* user to access data quickly and easily.

This Chapter in Review

- ▲ UNIX connectivity existed long before the Internet hit the scene. Even as the Internet explodes, UNIX tools provide essential for any serious Internet usage. For example, some older UNIX tools, such as **ftp** and **telnet**, still are valuable Internet tools.

- ▲ The **ftp** command allows you to connect to a remote computer and to transfer files to and from it. Public Internet computers allow you to sign on via anonymous FTP, which means you don't need an existing account or password.

▲ The **telnet** command allows you to directly link to another Internet computer and run programs from it.

▲ The **archie** command allows you to search an **archie** server for files that are stored on public FTP sites.

▲ **Gopher** is both a client on your UNIX machine and a database somewhere on the Internet. **Gopher** servers contain vast amounts of information—much of it useful, some of it frivolous. Tools that allow you to search **gopher** servers include **veronica** and **jughead**.

▲ The World Wide Web, or WWW, is an attempt to create a worldwide hypertext system, where references from one document lead directly to another document. Documents can be WWW sites, **gopher** servers, Usenet newsgroups, or FTP sites.

▲ Several browsers allow you to netsurf the WWW. The most popular UNIX browser is *NCSA Mosaic for the X Window System.*

▪ APPENDIX A ▪
For More Information

This book is only the beginning of the journey, should you desire to advance your working knowledge of UNIX. This appendix lays out further sources of information.

Printed Documentation

If the documentation that came with computer systems were any good, there would be no reason for a book like this. Have you browsed through the documentation that came with your UNIX system? Ouch.

This documentation serves its purpose: To provide valuable information for the system administrator. The purpose of this documentation is not to provide illumination for the end user. While some system-specific information can be found only in the documentation, the vast amount of it is technical information geared toward the advanced user. Approach the documentation with a grain of salt: Don't feel inadequate if you don't understand it fully.

Online-Manual Pages

One of the neater UNIX commands is **man**, which displays information about UNIX commands.

There's not a lot to the **man** command (as you'll see from Table A.1, the Command Reference for the **man** command)—essentially, it displays an *online manual page* about specific UNIX commands. It will not display information about practices and procedures, nor will it display information about specific UNIX topics, like *multitasking* or *processes*. Still, it's quite useful for displaying a *lot* of information about specific commands.

Unfortunately, the **man** command is not fully implemented on some UNIX system, and not at all on other UNIX systems. If you have it, great; if not, lobby your system administrator.

For more information on the **man** command itself (and assuming you have access to it, of course), use the following command line:

```
$ man man
```

TABLE A.1 COMMAND REFERENCE FOR THE MAN COMMAND

man *command*

PURPOSE
The **man** command displays the online manual page for a command.

OPTIONS
None.

Books

As you can tell by a visit to your local bookstore, there are a ton of titles devoted to the UNIX operating system, as well as the Internet. However, when you start looking at the titles and the tables of contents, you realize that most of them are meant for advanced users and/or system administrators. By contrast, the book in your hands is one of the few books devoted to anyone other than advanced users and/or system

▼

administrators, and perhaps the only one devoted solely to the UNIX neophyte. (It's also one of the few that covers networking and communications for the UNIX user.)

At this point in your UNIX education, though, you may be ready to move on to more advanced tomes. Here are some titles that should aid you in your higher education.

General Titles

UNIX Fundamentals: UNIX Basics Kevin Reichard, MIS:Press, 1994. This book is the first in this series, and it lays out the basics of UNIX usage. If you're still puzzled by some aspects of UNIX usage, this is a good place to start.

UNIX Fundamentals: UNIX for DOS/*Windows* Users Kevin Reichard, MIS:Press, 1994. The second in the UNIX Fundamentals series, this book is geared for those with some experience in the DOS and *Windows* world, and who want to transfer some of that experience to the UNIX world.

Teach Yourself UNIX Kevin Reichard and Eric F. Johnson, MIS:Press, 1992. This introduction to the UNIX operating system is meant for a more advanced computer user, but still has enough details for the learning beginner. Most of the commands listed in this work are more fully explained in Teach Yourself UNIX, while the underlying concepts of UNIX are explained in depth.

UNIX in Plain English Kevin Reichard and Eric F. Johnson, MIS:Press, 1994. This reference works focuses on in-depth explanations of the important UNIX commands. Definitely the book to be sitting next to your terminal for a quick reference.

X Window System

Using X Eric F. Johnson and Kevin Reichard, MIS:Press, 1992. This book explains the basics of X Window System usage and configuration. While X Window can be complex, even a beginner is able to handle the very elementary configuration details, as explained in this book.

▼

The Internet

There are over 100 Internet books on the market. Most are blather and blatant rip-offs, repackaging public information already contained on the Internet. There are a few gems, however, so if you want to expand your Internet knowledge, you should check out these titles.

The Whole Internet User's Guide and Catalog Ed Krol, O'Reilly & Associates, Inc., second edition, 1994. One of the first Internet guides and still one of the best, Krol's guide covers the Internet in a lot of depth, yet doesn't descend into jargon or obscure references.

Using UUCP and Usenet Grace Todino and Dale Dougherty, O'Reilly & Associates, Inc., 1986. A good introduction to UUCP and the Usenet.

Online Sources

As you might expect from a computer system with networking built in, there are many online resources you can tap. The greatest amount of information is carried over the Usenet.

Usenet UNIX Newsgroups

There are a ton of Usenet newsgroups, as you've learned by now. (A selected list appears in Appendix B.) Be warned that many of the newsgroups are geared toward experts of one sort or another, and that some may feel that participation by a UNIX neophyte is not exactly welcome. Asking a general question of a set of UNIX experts is generally met by disdain, rudeness, and techie arrogance. (The exception is the *comp.unix.questions* newsgroup, which is designed specifically for beginners.) If you choose to participate in a specialized topic, you're on your own; the advice from these quarters is to monitor the newsgroups and to pick up useful knowledge in that fashion. General questions are best asked of your system administrator or other UNIX users in your area.

▼

CompuServe

There are hundreds of forums on CompuServe, but an especially friendly forum for UNIX beginners is the UNIX Forum. Topics in this forum include: Forum Info/General, New to UNIX, Communications, Networking, Applications, UNIX OS Topics, DOS under UNIX, and GUI and X Window. This forum also contains software libraries. (To get to the UNIX Forum, type GO UNIX.)

In addition, there are forums maintained by several UNIX vendors that specialize in PC versions of UNIX, and the users on these forums generally have one foot in the DOS world and one foot in the UNIX world. If you need to combine the two worlds, you might want to check out the UnixWare (GO UNIXWARE) or SCO (GO SCO) forums for some advice and pertinent software libraries.

And don't forget the existence of CompuServe forums dedicated to certain portions of UNIX usage. For instance, there's an Internet forum (GO INET) that you might find useful if you want to follow-up on Chapter 9.

▪ APPENDIX B ▪
A Sampling of Usenet Newsgroups

At this time, there are over 1,000 newsgroups on the Usenet. You obviously don't want to wade through all 1,000 newsgroups to find what you want. This appendix lists some of the more popular and mainstream newsgroups, chosen in an admittedly arbitrary fashion, since there's not enough space in this book to list *all* of the newsgroups. (For starters: There's no current list of alternative newsgroups. You're on your own when you wander through newsgroups like **alt.fetish**.) It's based on a list created by Gene Spafford (*spaf@cs.purdue.edu*) and maintained by David C Lawrence (*tale@uunet.uu.net*). The newsgroups are current as of August 1994. To get the latest list of all mainstream Usenet newsgroups, you can grab it from *pit-manager.mit.edu* in the **/pub** directory.

NEWSGROUP	AUDIENCE/PURPOSE
comp.ai	Artificial-intelligence discussions.
comp.ai.neural-nets	All aspects of neural networks.
comp.answers	Repository for periodic USENET articles. (Moderated.)
comp.apps.spreadsheets	Spreadsheets on various platforms.
comp.arch	Computer architecture.
comp.archives	Descriptions of public-access archives. (Moderated.)
comp.databases	Database and data-management issues and theory.
Comp.laser-printers	Laser printers, hardware, and software. (Moderated.)

comp.databases.sybase	Implementations of the SQL Server.
comp.emacs	Emacs editors of different flavors.
comp.fonts	Typefaces—design, conversion, use, etc.
comp.graphics	Computer graphics, art, animation, and image processing.
comp.graphics.animation	Technical aspects of computer animation.
comp.infosystem	Any discussion about information systems.
comp.infosystems.gopher	Discussion of the **gopher** information service.
comp.infosystems.interpedia	The Internet Encyclopedia.
comp.infosystems.wais	The Z39.50-based WAIS full-text search system.
comp.infosystems.www	The World Wide Web information system.
comp.infosystems.www.misc	Miscellaneous World Wide Web discussion.
comp.infosystems.www.providers	WWW provider issues (info providers).
comp.infosystems.www.users	WWW user issues (**mosaic**, **lynx**, etc.).
comp.internet.library	Discussing electronic libraries. (Moderated.)
comp.lang.c	Discussion about C.
comp.lang.c++	The object-oriented C++ language.
comp.lang.perl	Discussion of Larry Wall's Perl system.
comp.lang.tcl	The Tcl programming language and related tools.
ccomp.mail.elm	Discussion and fixes for the **elm** mail system.

comp.mail.headers	Gatewayed from the Internet header-people list.
comp.mail.maps	Various maps, including UUCP maps. (Moderated.)
comp.mail.mh	The UCI version of the Rand Message Handling system.
comp.mail.mime	Multipurpose Internet Mail Extensions of RFC 1341.
comp.mail.misc	General discussions about computer mail.
comp.mail.mush	The Mail User's Shell (MUSH).
comp.mail.pine	The PINE mail user agent.
comp.mail.sendmail	Configuring and using the BSD sendmail agent.
comp.mail.uucp	Mail in the UUCP network environment.
comp.misc	General topics about computers not covered elsewhere.
comp.multimedia	Interactive multimedia technologies of all kinds.
comp.newprod	Announcements of new products of interest. (Moderated.)
comp.os.linux.admin	Installing and administering Linux systems.
comp.os.linux.announce	Announcements important to the Linux community. (Moderated.)
comp.os.linux.development	Ongoing work on the Linux operating system.
comp.os.linux.help	Questions and advice about Linux.
comp.os.linux.misc	Linux-specific topics not covered by other groups.
comp.os.mach	The Mach operating system from CMU and other places.

comp.programming	Programming issues that transcend languages and operating systems.
comp.protocols.ppp	Discussion of the Internet Point to Point Protocol.
comp.protocols.tcp-ip	TCP and IP network protocols.
comp.publish.cdrom.hardware	Hardware used in publishing with CD-ROM.
comp.publish.cdrom.multimedia	Software for multimedia authoring and publishing.
comp.publish.cdrom.software	Software used in publishing with CD-ROM.
comp.publish.prepress	Electronic prepress.
comp.risks	Risks to the public from computers and users. (Moderated.)
comp.security.unix	Discussion of UNIX security.
comp.society	The impact of technology on society. (Moderated.)
comp.society.privacy	Effects of technology on privacy. (Moderated.)
comp.sources.sun	Software for Sun workstations. (Moderated.)
comp.sources.unix	Postings of complete, UNIX-oriented sources. (Moderated.)
comp.sources.x	Software for the X Window System. (Moderated.)
comp.sys.hp.hpux	Issues pertaining to HP-UX and 9000 series computers.
comp.sys.misc	Discussion about computers of all kinds.
comp.sys.ncr	Discussion about NCR computers.
comp.sys.next.advocacy	The NeXT religion.

comp.sys.next.hardware	Discussing the physical aspects of NeXT computers.
comp.sys.next.marketplace	NeXT hardware, software, and jobs.
comp.sys.next.misc	General discussion about the NeXT computer system.
comp.sys.sgi.announce	Announcements for the SGI community. (Moderated.)
comp.sys.sgi.apps	Applications that run on the Iris.
comp.sys.sgi.audio	Audio on SGI systems.
comp.sys.sgi.graphics	Graphics packages and issues on SGI machines.
comp.sys.sgi.hardware	Base systems and peripherals for SGI Iris computers.
comp.sys.sgi.misc	General discussion about Silicon Graphics machines.
comp.sys.sun.announce	Sun announcements and Sunergy mailings. (Moderated.)
comp.sys.sun.apps	Software applications for Sun computer systems.
comp.sys.sun.hardware	Sun Microsystems hardware.
comp.sys.sun.misc	Miscellaneous discussions about Sun products.
comp.sys.sun.wanted	People looking for Sun products and support.
comp.sys.unisys	Sperry, Burroughs, Convergent, and Unisys systems.
comp.unix.admin	Administering a UNIX-based system.
comp.unix.advocacy	Arguments for and against UNIX and UNIX versions.
comp.unix.aix	IBM's version of UNIX.
comp.unix.aux	The version of UNIX for Apple Macintosh II computers.

comp.unix.bsd	Discussion of Berkeley Software Distribution UNIX.
comp.unix.dos-under-unix	MS-DOS running under UNIX by whatever means.
comp.unix.large	UNIX on mainframes and in large networks.
comp.unix.misc	Various topics that don't fit other groups.
comp.unix.osf.misc	Various aspects of Open Software Foundation products.
comp.unix.osf.osf1	The Open Software Foundation's OSF/1.
comp.unix.pc-clone.16bit	UNIX on 286 architectures.
comp.unix.pc-clone.32bit	UNIX on 386 and 486 architectures.
comp.unix.programmer	Q&A for people programming under UNIX.
comp.unix.questions	UNIX neophytes group.
comp.unix.shell	Using and programming the UNIX shell.
comp.unix.sys3	System III UNIX discussions.
comp.unix.sys5.misc	Versions of System V that predate Release 3.
comp.unix.sys5.r3	Discussing System V Release 3.
comp.unix.sys5.r4	Discussing System V Release 4.
comp.unix.ultrix	Discussion about DEC's Ultrix.
comp.unix.unixware	Discussion about Novell's UnixWare products.
comp.unix.user-friendly	Discussion of UNIX user-friendliness.
comp.unix.xenix.misc	General discussions regarding XENIX (except SCO).

comp.unix.xenix.sco	XENIX versions from the Santa Cruz Operation.
comp.windows.open-look	Discussion about the Open Look GUI.
comp.windows.x	Discussion about the X Window System.
comp.windows.x.announce	X Consortium announcements. (Moderated.)
comp.windows.x.apps	Getting and using, not programming, applications for X.
comp.windows.x.i386unix	The XFree86 window system and others.
comp.windows.x.intrinsics	Discussion of the X toolkit.
misc.activism.progressive	Information for Progressive activists. (Moderated.)
misc.answers	Repository for periodic USENET articles. (Moderated.)
misc.books.technical	Discussion of books about technical topics.
misc.consumers	Consumer interests, product reviews, etc.
misc.entrepreneurs	Discussion on operating a business.
misc.fitness	Physical fitness, exercise, body-building, etc.
misc.health.alternative	Alternative, complementary, and holistic health care.
misc.invest	Investments and the handling of money.
misc.jobs.offered	Announcements of positions available.
misc.kids	Children, their behavior, and activities.

misc.kids.computer	The use of computers by children.
misc.legal	Legalities and the ethics of law.
misc.misc	Various discussions not fitting in any other group.
misc.rural	Devoted to issues concerning rural living.
misc.taxes	Tax laws and advice.
misc.writing	Discussion of writing in all of its forms.
news.announce.important	General announcements of interest to all. (Moderated.)
news.announce.newgroups	Calls for newgroups and announcements of same. (Moderated.)
news.announce.newusers	Explanatory postings for new users. (Moderated.)
news.answers	Repository for periodic USENET articles. (Moderated.)
news.groups	Discussions and lists of newsgroups.
news.groups.questions	Where can I find talk about topic X?
news.groups.reviews	What is going on in group or mailing list named X? (Moderated.)
news.misc	Discussions of USENET itself.
news.newsites	Postings of new site announcements.
news.newusers.questions	Q&A for users new to the Usenet.
news.software.nn	Discussion about the nn newsreader package.
news.software.readers	Discussion of software used to read network news.
rec.answers	Repository for periodic USENET articles. (Moderated.)

rec.antiques	Discussing antiques and vintage items.
rec.aquaria	Keeping fish and aquaria as a hobby.
rec.arts.animation	Discussion of various kinds of animation.
rec.arts.bodyart	Tattoos and body decoration discussions.
rec.arts.bonsai	Dwarfish trees and shrubbery.
rec.arts.books	Books of all genres, and the publishing industry.
rec.arts.cinema	Discussion of the art of cinema. (Moderated.)
rec.arts.comics.creative	Encouraging good superhero-style writing.
rec.arts.comics.strips	Discussion of short-form comics.
rec.arts.comics.xbooks	The Mutant Universe of Marvel Comics.
rec.arts.dance	Any aspects of dance not covered in another newsgroup.
rec.arts.fine	Fine arts and artists.
rec.arts.movies.reviews	Reviews of movies. (Moderated.)
rec.arts.sf.science	Real and speculative aspects of SF science.
rec.arts.sf.written	Discussion of written science fiction and fantasy.
rec.arts.startrek.info	Information about the universe of Star Trek. (Moderated.)
rec.arts.startrek.misc	General discussions of Star Trek.
rec.arts.theatre	Discussion of all aspects of stage work and theatre.
rec.arts.tv	The boob tube, its history, and past and current shows.

rec.arts.tv.mst3k	For fans of Mystery Science Theater 3000.
rec.arts.wobegon	"A Prairie Home Companion" radio show discussion.
rec.audio.opinion	Everybody's two bits on audio in your home.
rec.autos.tech	Technical aspects of automobiles, et. al.
rec.backcountry	Activities in the Great Outdoors.
rec.bicycles.misc	General discussion of bicycling.
rec.birds	Hobbyists interested in bird watching.
rec.boats	Hobbyists interested in boating.
rec.climbing	Climbing techniques, competition announcements, etc.
rec.collecting	Discussion among collectors of many things.
rec.crafts.brewing	The art of making beers and meads.
rec.crafts.winemaking	The tasteful art of making wine.
rec.folk-dancing	Folk dances, dancers, and dancing.
rec.food.cooking	Food, cooking, cookbooks, and recipes.
rec.food.drink	Wines and spirits.
rec.food.drink.beer	All things beer.
rec.food.drink.coffee	The making and drinking of coffee.
rec.food.historic	The history of food-making arts.
rec.food.recipes	Recipes for interesting food and drink. (Moderated.)
rec.food.veg	Vegetarians.
rec.games.backgammon	Discussion of the game of backgammon.
rec.games.chess	Chess and computer chess.

rec.gardens	Gardening, methods, and results.
rec.guns	Discussions about firearms. (Moderated.)
rec.mag	Magazine summaries, tables of contents, etc.
rec.music.a-cappella	Vocal music without instrumental accompaniment.
rec.music.afro-latin	Music with Afro-Latin, African, and Latin influences.
rec.music.beatles	Postings about the Fab Four and their music.
rec.music.bluenote	Discussion of jazz, blues, and related types of music.
rec.music.cd	CDs—availability and other discussions.
rec.music.classical	Discussion about classical music.
rec.music.classical.guitar	Classical music performed on guitar.
rec.music.classical.performing	Performing classical (including early) music.
rec.music.dylan	Discussion of Bob's works and music.
rec.music.early	Discussion of preclassical European music.
rec.music.folk	Folks discussing folk music of various sorts.
rec.music.funky	Funk, rap, hip-hop, house, soul, and related.
rec.music.gaffa	Discussion of Kate Bush and other alternative music. (Moderated.)
rec.music.gdead	A group for (Grateful) Dead-heads.

rec.music.industrial	Discussion of all industrial-related music styles.
rec.music.makers	For performers and their discussions.
rec.music.marketplace	Records, tapes, and CDs: wanted, for sale, etc.
rec.music.misc	Music lovers' group.
rec.music.phish	Discussing the musical group Phish.
rec.music.reggae	Roots, Rockers, Dancehall Reggae.
rec.music.rem	The musical group R.E.M.
rec.music.reviews	Reviews of music of all genres and mediums. (Moderated.)
rec.nude	Hobbyists interested in naturist/ nudist activities.
rec.org.mensa	Talking with members of the high IQ society Mensa.
rec.org.sca	Society for Creative Anachronism.
rec.outdoors.fishing	All aspects of sport and commercial fishing.
rec.outdoors.fishing.fly	Fly fishing in general.
rec.pets	Pets, pet care, and household animals in general.
rec.pets.cats	Discussion about domestic cats.
rec.pets.dogs	Any and all subjects relating to dogs as pets.
rec.photo	Hobbyists interested in photography.
rec.puzzle	Puzzles, problems, and quizzes.
rec.radio.shortwave	Shortwave radio enthusiasts.
rec.railroad	For fans of real trains, ferroequinologists.

rec.skate	Ice skating and roller skating.
rec.skiing.announce	FAQ, competition results, and automated snow reports. (Moderated.)
rec.sport.baseball	Discussion about baseball.
rec.sport.baseball.fantasy	Rotisserie (fantasy) baseball play.
rec.sport.basketball.college	Hoops on the collegiate level.
rec.sport.basketball.pro	Talk of professional basketball.
rec.sport.basketball.women	Women's basketball at all levels.
rec.sport.cricket	Discussion about the sport of cricket.
rec.sport.football.college	U.S.-style college football.
rec.sport.football.fantasy	Rotisserie (fantasy) football play.
rec.sport.football.pro	U.S.-style professional football.
rec.sport.hockey	Discussion about ice hockey.
rec.sport.pro-wrestling	Discussion about professional wrestling.
rec.sport.tennis	Things related to the sport of tennis.
rec.toys.lego	Discussion of Lego, Duplo, and compatible toys.
rec.toys.misc	Discussion of toys that lack a specific newsgroup.
rec.travel	Traveling all over the world.
rec.woodworking	Hobbyists interested in woodworking.
sci.aeronautics	The science of aeronautics and related technology. (Moderated.)
sci.agriculture	Farming, agriculture, and related topics.
sci.agriculture.beekeeping	Beekeeping, bee-culture, and hive products.

sci.answers	Repository for periodic USENET articles. (Moderated.)
sci.anthropology	All aspects of studying humankind.
sci.aquaria	Only scientifically oriented postings about aquaria.
sci.archaeology	Studying antiquities of the world.
sci.astro	Astronomy discussions and information.
sci.bio	Biology and related sciences.
sci.chem	Chemistry and related sciences.
sci.cognitive	Perception, memory, judgment, and reasoning.
sci.econ	The science of economics.
sci.edu	The science of education.
sci.electronics	Circuits, theory, electrons, and discussions.
sci.engr	Technical discussions about engineering tasks.
sci.environment	Discussions about the environ-. ment and ecology.
sci.logic	Logic—math, philosophy, and computationalaspects.
sci.misc	Short-lived discussions on subjects in the sciences.
sci.physics	Physical laws, properties, etc.
sci.psychology	Topics related to psychology.
sci.space.news	Announcements of space-related news items. (Moderated.)
sci.space.policy	Discussions about space policy.
sci.space.science	Space and planetary science and related technical work. (Moderated.)

soc.answers	Repository for periodic USENET articles. (Moderated.)
soc.bi	Discussions of bisexuality.
soc.couples	Discussions for couples (cf. soc.singles).
soc.couples.intercultural	Intercultural and interracial relationships.
soc.culture.celtic	Irish, Scottish, Breton, Cornish, Manx, and Welsh.
soc.feminism	Discussion of feminism and feminist issues. (Moderated.)
soc.history	Discussions of things historical.
soc.libraries.talk	Discussing all aspects of libraries.
soc.men	Issues related to men, their problems, and relationships.
soc.misc	Socially oriented topics not in other groups.
soc.penpals	In search of net.friendships.
soc.politics	Political problems, systems, solutions. (Moderated.)
soc.religion.christian.bible-study	Examining the Holy Bible. (Moderated.)
soc.religion.gnosis	Gnosis, marifat, jnana, and direct sacred experience. (Moderated.)
soc.religion.islam	Discussions of the Islamic faith. (Moderated.)
soc.religion.quaker	The Religious Society of Friends.
soc.rights.human	Human rights and activism (e.g., Amnesty International).
soc.singles	Newsgroup for single people, their activities, etc.
soc.women	Issues related to women, their problems, and relationships.

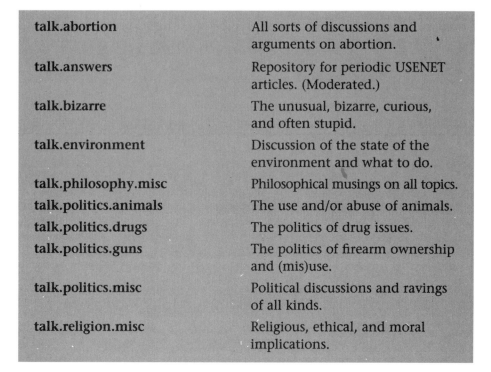

talk.abortion	All sorts of discussions and arguments on abortion.
talk.answers	Repository for periodic USENET articles. (Moderated.)
talk.bizarre	The unusual, bizarre, curious, and often stupid.
talk.environment	Discussion of the state of the environment and what to do.
talk.philosophy.misc	Philosophical musings on all topics.
talk.politics.animals	The use and/or abuse of animals.
talk.politics.drugs	The politics of drug issues.
talk.politics.guns	The politics of firearm ownership and (mis)use.
talk.politics.misc	Political discussions and ravings of all kinds.
talk.religion.misc	Religious, ethical, and moral implications.

▪ GLOSSARY ▪

absolute pathname	The full name of a file, from the root directory on through each subdirectory.
account	Information about your UNIX usage, such as your username and the way your terminal is configured.
address	The name of a computer on the network or the name of the entire computer system, used in communications and electronic mail. An address can also refer to someone's personal electronic-mail address, which can be written in Internet or Usenet format.
anonymous	ftp Logging on a remote system anonymously to retrieve files (that is, logging in a system without having an account already set up on the system); this method involves limited access to the remote system.
append	Attach characters to the end of an existing file.
application	A program that performs a specific task, such as a text editor or a database manager.
archive	A file that can contain one or more files, serving as a backup (usually on tape) to files on a hard drive.
arguments	Additions to a command that slightly change the result of the command, either by adding options or specifying filenames.
ASCII	American Standard Code for Information Interchange; a standard format used to store basic alphabetic characters and numerals in a way that any computer—running UNIX or another operating system—can read the file.

▼

background	State where commands are run without the full attention and resources of the system; when the commands finish running, the user is notified. Background commands are run from a command line that ends with an ampersand (&).
Bourne shell	See *shell*.
C	Programming language that serves as a basis of UNIX; in addition, most UNIX programs are written in C or its successor, C++.
C shell	See *shell*.
command	A direct instruction to the computer system.
command line	The combination of a command and any arguments to the command.
command prompt	A specific character used by a specific shell in conjunction with the cursor to tell you that the system is ready for a command.
compressed file	A file that has been shrunk so it can more quickly be transferred from computer to computer.
current directory	Your current position on the directory tree.
cursor	A blinking line or square on the monitor that tells you the system is waiting for a command.
default	A state or value assumed when no other is present.
device	A physical device attached to the computer system, such as a modem or tape drive.
directory	The means for storing files or other directories, analogous to a folder in a file cabinet.
DOS	See *MS-DOS*.
dot file	See *hidden file*.
electronic mail	The electronic equivalent of mail: text messages sent over the UNIX network, either from within the system or from outside the system.
encryption	A way of encoding a file so that it cannot be read by other users.

▼

environment	Information that determines your UNIX usage and system configuration, as stored in your **.profile** file or set during your computing session.
error message	A message from the computer system informing you that it cannot perform a specific function.
Ethernet	A networking protocol used to link computers of all sorts, including UNIX-based computers.
executable file	A file containing a program.
FAQ (Frequently Asked Questions)	A list of commonly asked questions on a specific topic (and their answers, of course) dissemonated via the Internet.
field	A vertical column of data from a structured data file, with all of the entries of the same type.
file	The mechanism for storing information on a UNIX system: a set of characters (called bytes) referenced by its filename.
filename	The name for a file.
filesystem	The method used in UNIX to organize files and directories: A root directory contains several subdirectories, and these subdirectories in turn may contain further subdirectories.
foreground	Commands that have the full attention of the system and do not return control of the system to the user until the command is complete. In UNIX, the default is to run commands in the foreground.
freeware	Software created by others and then given away to the computing community at large.
graphical interface	A graphical display on the monitor, with windows, scrollbars, and icons.
group	A defined set of users.
header	Beginning of an electronic-mail message that contains information about where the message is from and the route it took to you.

▼

hidden files	UNIX system files that are used for standard housekeeping chores; the filenames begin with a period (.) and are not listed with the **ls** command. Sometimes these hidden files are called *dot files*.
home directory	A directory where your own files are stored, and where you are placed after you login the system.
hostname	The name of your UNIX system.
HTML	HyperText Markup Language; the format for documents available via the Word Wide Web.
icon	A graphical representation of a program or file.
inbox	The storage area for electronic mail that has not been read.
Internet	The umbrella name for a group of computer networks that distribute electronic mail and newsgroups around the world.
keyboard	The big thing you type on to provide input to the computer.
Korn shell	See *shell*.
link	A file that serves as a reference to another file. Many users can use the same files, making it appear as though they each have their own copy of the file.
login	To announce your presence to the system by entering your username and password.
login script	A script, usually contained in **.login**, that contains basic information about your UNIX usage; this script runs every time you login.
logname	The name the UNIX system uses to keep track of you. Also known as *username*.
machine	Another way of referring to a UNIX system.
mail reader	UNIX program that sends and receives your electronic mail. Popular examples include **mail**, **mailx**, and **elm**.

▼

mailbox	File in your home directory that stores your mail.
Meta key	A specified key used in conjunction with other keys to create additional key combinations. On most keyboards, the **Alt** key is really the **Meta** key.
Microsoft *Windows*	A graphical interface that runs on top of MS-DOS.
modem	A piece of hardware that allows computers to communicate via telephone lines.
monitor	That big ol' thing sitting on your desk that looks like a television on steroids.
multiprocessing	When more than one task can be performed simultaneously by the operating system. UNIX is a *multiprocessing* operating system.
multitasking	When more than one task can be performed simultaneously by the operating system. UNIX is a *multitasking* operating system.
multiuser	When more than one user can be using the same computer system. UNIX is a *multiuser* operating system.
MS-DOS	An operating system used by most PCs.
networking	Connecting one computer system to another computer system by direct wiring or phone lines.
newsgroup	Contributions from a variety of users, centered around various topics. The Usenet carries more than 1,400 newsgroups.
online manual page	Documentation for your system stored within files on the system, accessed with the **man** command.
operating system	A program that controls all actions of the computer hardware. UNIX is an operating system.
option	Characters that modify the default behavior of a command.
ordinary file	A file that is, well, ordinary, containing data or programs, with no special characters.
OSF/Motif	Created by the Open Software Foundation, Motif is actually many things—but for you, the

229
▼

▼

	most important thing is that it defines a look and feel for the graphical interface. Based on the X Window System.
owner	The user with the ability to set permissions for a file.
paging	Memory-management system where entire chunks of the UNIX system's RAM are switched back and forth between the hard disk. This situation occurs when there's not enough RAM to serve the needs of all users.
parent directory	The directory containing a subdirectory.
password	A unique set of character that the UNIX system uses to verify your existence when you want to login the system.
permissions	A security tool to determine who can access a file.
pipe	A conduit between two commands, which tells the second command to use the output from the first command as input.
port	There are two meanings to *port*, and both are used in discussions of UNIX communications. In this book, *port* was used in the context of a request when connecting to a remote system. Here, *port* refers to a specific Internet application on the remote machine.
post	To contribute an article to a newsgroup.
process	Essentially, a program running on the computer.
process ID (PID)	Number assigned by the system to a command.
program	A set of instructions for the computer to carry out.
prompt	See *command prompt*.
redirection	Changing the standard input/output; for instance, saving output to a file instead of printing it to the screen.
relative pathname	A filename in relation to the current directory position.

▼

▼

root directory	The top-most directory on the directory tree; every directory on a UNIX system is a subdirectory of the root directory. Indicated in all pathnames as a slash (/).
root user	The user who can do just about anything possible within the UNIX operating system. Also referred to as the **superuser**.
server	A computer that supplies files and services to other computers.
shell	Software that acts as a buffer between you and the operating system. There are many different UNIX shells—the Bourne shell, the Korn shell, and the C shell, for example.
shell script	A text file that serves as a set of instructions for the shell.
signature	A file that's attached to your mail or Usenet postings. Typically, this file is short and contains information about you—corporate address, e-mail address, and so on.
smiley	Stupid symbols that allow you to excuse away rudeness.
special device files	Files that represent physical parts of the UNIX system, such as tape drives or terminals.
standard input/output	The UNIX method of processing commands: The standard input comes from the keyboard, and the output goes to the screen.
states	Different levels that a UNIX system runs in, ranging from a single-user state to a multiuser state.
subdirectories	A directory contained within another directory. In UNIX, every directory is a subdirectory of the root directory.
swapping	Situation where UNIX processes are sent from RAM to a hard disk for temporary storage. This arises because of a shortage of available RAM in the system.

▼

system administrator	Your hero/heroine—the person responsible for running and maintaining the UNIX system.
terminal	A monitor, keyboard, perhaps a mouse, and perhaps a CPU.
text-based interface	An interface where only characters, and not graphics, are used.
text editor	UNIX commands that create and edit text files. These include **vi** and **emacs**.
text file	A file containing only ASCII characters and no special characters. A text file can be read by any program.
UNIX	An operating system that supports more than one user and can perform more than one command at a time—and, of course, the greatest operating system in the world.
Usenet	Public collection of computers that is one component of the Internet. The Usenet is best known for distributing newsgroups.
username	The name that the UNIX system uses to keep track of you. Also known as *logname*.
UUCP	A suite of commands that manage connectivity between your computer and other computers that support UUCP.
variable	A symbol or character that has different meanings based on context and specific usage.
wildcard	Special characters within a filename that tells the shell to look for all files with similar filenames.
window manager	A program within the X Window System that controls the look and feel of the interface.
Windows	See *Microsoft Windows*.
working directory	See *current directory*.
workstation	A computer optimized for running UNIX. Sun SPARCstations and IBM RS/6000s are *workstations*.

▼

X terminal   A terminal that runs only the X Window System and draws most of its computing power from the network.

X Window System   Graphical windowing system used for building graphical interfaces, like Motif.

xterm   Popular X Window System program that provides a command-line interface to the UNIX operating system.

▪INDEX▪

▪C▪

CERN, 192, 196, 197

Chimera, 197

client/server, 11

   defined, 11

compress command, 167

CompuServe, 127, 128, 207

cu command, 124, 126-137

   command, 134-135

   and CompuServe ,127, 128

   and Delphi, 127

   and Hayes commands, 129

   and MCI Mail, 128-132, 133, 134

   problems with, 136

   and UUCP, 132-133

▪D▪

Digital Equipment Corp., 14, 96

domain names, 17

▪E▪

electronic mail, 8, 9, 10, 11, 12, 14-15, 16, 17, 18, 19, 23-57, 89, 181-183, 200

▼

■F■

▼

▪J▪

▪L▪

▪M▪

▪N▪

▼

eliminating newsgroups, 111-113

modes, 109, 111

status line, 110

options, 110-111

▪O▪

online-manual pages, 203-204

▪P▪

pack command, 167

perlWWW, 197

pnews command, 113-114

Postnews command, 113-114

Pretty Good Privacy (PGP), 75

privacy, 74-75

▪R▪

rcp command, 158-159

readnews newsreader, 102

rlogin command, 156-157, 158

rn newsreader, 102-107, 109, 111

adding newsgroups, 111-113

commands, 103, 105-106

▼

trn newsreader, 102

▪U▪

UNIX, 1, 2, 3, 4, 5, 9, 11, 14, 15, 17-18, 20, 24, 25, 26, 28, 29, 33, 34, 35, 36, 40, 42-43, 44, 45, 49, 50, 52, 53, 54, 55, 61, 67, 71, 72, 75, 78, 79, 80, 82, 85, 88, 89, 94, 95, 96, 100, 102, 103, 112, 116, 119, 120, 124, 126, 127, 128, 132, 134, 138, 139, 140, 146, 155, 156, 162, 163, 164, 165, 167, 169, 173, 176, 185, 196, 199, 203, 204, 205, 206

    BSD 24, 127, 155

    and compressed files, 167

    and electronic mail, 14

    and hardware, 82

    history, 9, 24

    System V, 24, 25

uncompress command, 167-168, 193

Uniform Resource Locator, (URL) 193

unpack command, 168

Usenet, 15-16, 78, 79, 94-121, 136, 192, 195, 206

    acronyms, 101-102

    addresses, 15-16

    conventions, 101-102

    drawbacks, 120-121

    etiquette, 114-115

▼